THE BASS BOOK

TONY BACON & BARRY MOORHOUSE

The Bass Book
An illustrated history of the bass guitar
By Tony Bacon & Barry Moorhouse

GPI Books
An imprint of Miller Freeman Books, San Francisco

Published in the UK by Balafon Books, an imprint of Outline Press Ltd,
115J Cleveland Street, London W1P 5PN, England.

First American Edition 1995
Published in the United States by Miller Freeman Books,
600 Harrison Street, San Francisco, CA 94107
Publishers of GPI Books and *Bass Player* magazine
A member of the United Newspapers Group

ISBN 0-87930-368-9

Printed in China

Art Director: Nigel Osborne
Design: Sally Stockwell
Editor: Roger Cooper
Typesetting by Type Technique, London
Print and origination by Regent Publishing Services

96 97 98 5 4 3 2

CONTENTS

Electric Bass . .
delivers that deep, powerful
bass sound every band needs

With leatherette-covered chipboard case. Strings set
low for fast-action playing. Rosewood fingerboard
with 4-octave range. Flat-wound strings, single pickup. Tone, volume controls. Steel rods reinforce neck.
Black semi-solid body of hardwood and composition-
wood. Instructions. About 43x13x2 in.
57 G 1444L—Shpg. wt. 24 lbs. $5 mo. Cash $79.95

$79.95

Extra Electric-bass Strings. Set of 4. Flat-wound.
57 G 3627—Shipping wt. 4 oz. . . . . Set $3.95

INTRODUCTION

We are proud to bring you the first book to tell the story of the electric bass guitar. Modern music would sound completely different had it not been for this remarkable musical tool, the most subversive new instrument of the 20th century.

With so much attention leveled at the guitar today it is astonishing how little effort has been afforded to the history of the bass. We've uncovered some fascinating tales: how Leo Fender's ground-breaking Precision model was described in the 1950s as anything from "a sensational instrumental innovation" to "an amplified plink-plonk"; how Alembic grew from the vision of a hallucinogenic manufacturer to establish a radical new look and sound; how Ned Steinberger turned conventional design on its head with his graphite "superwood" basses. And that's just for starters.

At the same time, we found that the story of the bass guitar is inextricably linked to its players. Bassists have constantly inspired and driven makers to produce new, different and exciting instrumental variations – from extra low-tuned strings to fretless fingerboards – that in turn have stimulated fresh musical routes and diversions.

You'll also find inside an unrivaled gallery of specially commissioned photographs of rare and beautiful bass guitars owned by players such as Jack Bruce, Stanley Clarke, John Entwistle, Mark King, Paul McCartney, Marcus Miller and Pino Palladino.

Closing the book is a comprehensive reference section, a unique compendium detailing instruments from the world's leading bass manufacturers.

It was a pleasure to step out into the uncharted territory of bass guitar history, and we hope you enjoy what we brought back.

TONY BACON & BARRY MOORHOUSE, ENGLAND, JANUARY 1995

"Listen to modern music and you will find that the bass is one of the most important instruments, adding the deep, profound pulsations that are the heart and soul of true rhythm."
A GIBSON **guitar catalog** *DEFINES THE GROOVE … IN 1928*

"Those who were not sure if Leo Fender was crazy when he brought out the solidbody guitar were darn sure he was crazy when he came up with an electric bass. They were convinced that a person would have to be out of their mind to play that thing."
FENDER ASSOCIATE **Forrest White** *RECALLS THE 1950s*

"None of us wanted to be the bass player. In our minds it was the fat guy in the group nearly always played the bass, and he stood at the back. None of us wanted that, we wanted to be up front singing, looking good, to pull the birds."
Paul McCartney *BRINGS THE BASS FORWARD IN THE EARLY 1960s*

"Bass players were far more interested in a new, clear approach, whereas guitar players seemed satisfied with what they had."
Rick Turner *DESCRIBES ALEMBIC'S CUSTOMERS OF THE EARLY 1970s*

"The upright bass is a pain in the ass, it's just too much work for too little sound … No matter how loud you get you're not loud enough."
Jaco Pastorius *CHOOSES FRETLESS BASS GUITAR IN THE 1970s*

"A lot of people, including us, began to presume that everyone would be playing a headless bass in ten years of so. Of course that turned out not to be the case at all."
Ned Steinberger *GETS AHEAD IN THE 1980s*

"The electric bass is becoming more modernized all the time. They're building four-string, five-string, six-string, eight-string, fretless, piccolo and two-octave basses; basses with thick necks, thin necks and graphite necks, plastic bodies, wood bodies, *no* bodies."
Jeff Berlin *DECLARES THE STATE OF THE BASS IN 1984*

THIS PAGE: Gibson's first bass, pictured in a 1954 ad (top left), recalled the cumbersome double-bass that the electric bass guitar was supposed to replace. Perhaps Rickenbacker's 1957 promo photo (top center) of their new 4000 model was meant to underline its suitability for dance music? Ampeg were important during the early history of the bass, inventing the fretless bass guitar in 1966. Four Seasons bassist Joe Long (center, far left) demonstrates the fretted version in a 1960s Ampeg brochure. A rather more famous left-hander, Paul McCartney, is pictured (left) with his renowned Höfner 'violin bass', while bass player's bass player John Patitucci (near left, 1992) plays one of the latest six-string basses by Yamaha.

OPPOSITE PAGE: Leo Fender (top left) was the man without whom the electric bass would not have existed. Leo's workshop at G&L (right, center) is shown as it was on the day he died in 1991. Ned Steinberger (top right) re-invented the bass in the early 1980s with his mini-body, headless, plastic instrument. Ron Wickersham (bottom right) set up Alembic in the late 1960s with Rick Turner, becoming the most influential maker of high-end bass guitars in the world.

BELOW: A luscious example of Fender's work, this 1964 Jazz Bass is finished in a beautiful Teal Green custom color.

6

In the beginning...

THE MAN BEHIND THE BASS
LEO FENDER
PRESIDENT, G&L MUSIC SALES, INC.

G&L MUSIC SALES INC. 2548 E. FENDER AVE., UNIT G • FULLERTON CA 92631

Picture the American guitarist of the late 1940s. Maybe he's playing an acoustic guitar. More likely he's got an amplified guitar, especially if he's a bluesman or plays in a jazz outfit or a Western swing band. In a big band he'll need one just to compete with the volume of the rest of the players, although the big band era is fading and increasingly the work he gets is in smaller groups. One way of getting more work is to be able to play an additional instrument, but our guitarist is used to the size and comfort of his fretted instrument, and when he tries a double-bass he struggles to maintain accurate intonation on that big, fretless instrument (nicknamed the 'doghouse' because of its awkward size).

Now picture the double-bass player, also in America at the end of the 1940s. All around him the rhythm section is getting louder: the drum kit is growing in size in order to project the music's pulse, and guitarists have become accustomed to using the amplified electric guitars that first appeared in the previous decade. But our bass player enjoys no such technology: he's saddled with the unwieldy acoustic double-bass and is still having trouble being heard over the musical noise being generated by his fellow band members.

The double-bass has a long and distinguished history, with most experts dating it back to Europe in the early-1500s. Since then it developed as the largest and lowest-tuned member of the violin family. Its most important musical settings have been as the anchor at the bottom of the string section in the modern symphony orchestra, where it began to appear from the early 18th century, and in jazz groups where in America in the 1920s it took over from the tuba as the principal bass instrument and quickly spread to other popular music bands.

STRANGE NEW HYBRID

So when, against this background, the Fender Electric Instrument Co of Los Angeles, California, introduced a solidbody electric bass guitar toward the end of 1951, nobody really knew what to make of this strange new hybrid. It looked like a long-necked version of Fender's Telecaster solidbody electric guitar which the company had launched in 1950. But the Fender Precision Bass had four strings on a long neck, and was tuned like a double-bass in fourths to E-A-D-G, an octave below the lower four strings of a guitar. Those who saw this new instrument gazed at a peculiar, unfamiliar thing.

If Fender's idea for a bass guitar was new – not to say downright shocking – the idea of an amplified bass was somewhat longer in the tooth. Thirty years earlier in the 1920s Lloyd Loar, an engineer at the Gibson Mandolin-Guitar Co in Kalamazoo, Michigan, had experimented with a slimmed-down electric double-bass. In the 1930s the Rickenbacker outfit of California marketed a 'stick'-shaped electric upright bass, and in the same decade Regal of Chicago put out a big guitar-shaped upright electric. None of these efforts was commercially successful, and they could not have been helped in their efforts by the poor quality of amplification available at that time. It seemed that makers knew that bass players wanted a louder instrument but were having trouble finding a suitable way of helping them.

AMPLIFIED PEG

In the late 1940s New York bassist Everett Hull approached the problem from a more practical angle: take the existing bass, he reasoned, and amplify that. So he began to produce an amplification system for acoustic double-basses consisting of a microphone that fitted inside the bass via the pointed 'peg' or spike that supports the instrument at its base. This 'amplified peg' gave the company its name – Ampeg – and their adaptation of existing double-basses to amplified sound was a moderate success.

Four-string guitars had hit the North American market well in advance of Fender's 1951 Precision, although they were quite different in purpose. In the 1920s companies such as Gibson (again) and Martin of Nazareth, Pennsylvania, came up with the acoustic 'tenor guitar' (Rickenbacker and Vega later made electric versions). It certainly wasn't a bass guitar, but a guitar that sported four strings tuned C-D-G-A on a narrow neck so that banjo players would be encouraged to move from the old-guard banjo to the newly popular guitar.

Also worth noting is that Martin briefly called their Dreadnought six-string flat-top acoustics of the 1930s 'bass guitars', but only because these new large-bodied instruments had a more bassy tone than usual, as they had been designed to suit vocal accompaniment.

It turns out that the idea of a fretted bass wasn't new either. Ancient multi-string fretted bass instruments such as the bass lute and theorbo had existed at least as far back as the 1600s, while at the beginning of this century Gibson made their four-string fretted Mando Bass model in small numbers, for 20 years or so from the early-1910s. The company's 1928 catalog, for example, shows a tuxedoed musician playing the acoustic Mando Bass with a pick, and holding the instrument guitar-style across his body thanks to the support of a metal rod that protrudes from the lower side of the Mando Bass to rest on the floor. The instrument had a 2ft wide pear-shaped body, a round soundhole, four strings tuned E-A-D-G, a 42in scale-length (the average for a double-bass) and 17 frets.

"Listen to modern music as played for dance, concert, recording or radio and you will find that the bass is one of the most important instruments, adding to the ensemble the deep, profound pulsations that are the heart and soul of true rhythm," suggested Gibson's catalog in a timeless phrase. Gibson described the fretted Mando Bass as "unusually easy to play", but what they didn't tell the budding bassist of 1928 was that this $150 instrument did little to project its sound through the band and into the audience; consequently it was not a great success during its surprisingly long life.

There is even some evidence of an electric bass guitar pre-dating Fender's Precision. Paul Tutmarc, a Hawaiian guitar player and teacher based in Seattle, Washington, set up a company called Audiovox to manufacture a variety of electric instruments, including an electric bass guitar, in the 1930s. The Audiovox Model 736 Bass Fiddle is shown in their leaflet dating from around 1936: it has a roughly guitar-shaped walnut body with a single pickup and control knob on a pearloid pickguard, a neck with 16 frets, and a cord emerging from a socket on the upper side of the body. This was an astonishingly early electric bass guitar design, and Tutmarc must at least be noted as a man with remarkable foresight, if little commercial luck. Tutmarc's son, Bud, later marketed a very similar electric bass guitar, called the Serenader, through the L D Heater music distribution company of Portland, Oregon. Heater's undated flyer describes the $139.50 Serenader electric bass guitar as "designed to eliminate the bulkiness of a regular size bass viol" ('bass viol' being another term for double-bass). Bud claims that the Serenader bass guitar was launched in 1948, although there is no evidence to support this date.

Of course, none of this detracts from the huge significance and importance of Fender's introduction of their solidbody electric bass guitar in 1951. For the Audiovox and Serenader basses, even if they really were first, made no impact whatsoever on the market. In contrast, by the early-1960s Fender's electric bass guitar had become an industry standard.

PRECISION PRODUCTION

Leo Fender was born in the Fullerton/Anaheim area of Southern California in 1909. His parents were orange growers, and Leo was born in the barn that they had built (a house followed the next year). Despite working as an accountant, Leo loved electronics and ham radio, and as a young man built amplifiers and PA systems for outdoor sports events and other gatherings in the Orange County area.

In the late 1930s Leo opened a radio store, Fender Radio Service, in Fullerton. He sold electrical gear, records, musical instruments, PA systems and sheet music, as well as offering a repair service. This put Leo in touch with many local musicians. One in particular, violinist and lap-steel guitarist 'Doc' Kauffman, teamed up with Leo in a short-lived company and they began producing K&F (Kauffman and Fender) electric lap-steel guitars and amplifiers in 1945.

By February of the following year Kauffman had left, unsettled by Leo's workaholic methods and the precarious finances of the project, so Leo set up his own Fender Electric Instrument Co later in 1946. He continued to make and sell the

9

Fender Precision 1951 (left) Leo Fender's small Californian company started the entire bass guitar business with this revolutionary instrument, launched into a world of bulky double-basses and players who expected to spend the whole gig rooted to one position on stage. The Precision changed all that. Fender used the design of their just-released Telecaster electric guitar as a basis for the world's first commercially successful electric bass guitar, deriving the 'Precision' name from the fact that the new bass's fretted fingerboard offered musicians precise pitching. The rare example shown is one of the earliest known examples of the Fender Precision: the body is dated October 30th 1951 and the neck November 20th 1951.

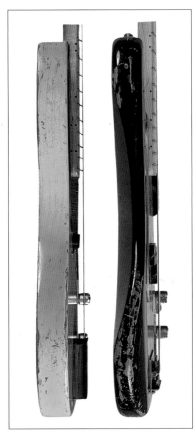

Fender flyer c1953 (above) At first Fender had to struggle to get across the idea that their strange new instrument was actually a useful musical tool.

10

Side views The Precision began life in 1951 with a squared, slab-sided body (right) like Fender's Telecaster guitar. However, when the company released its contoured Stratocaster guitar in 1954, the new curved-edge style, designed to offer the player a more comfortable feel, was also applied to the Precision Bass (far right).

Stringing (above) This view of the lower back of the 1951 Precision shows how until 1957 the strings were passed through the body, to be anchored at this point with four metal ferrules.

Fender Precision 1957 *(left) Note the new features introduced during 1957: a two-piece humbucking pickup, which replaced the earlier single-coil 'bar' type, and a much wider headstock. At this time Fender also briefly replaced the original pickguard with a gold-colored anodized aluminum guard. Collectors consider this combination of 1950s features — contoured body, one-piece maple neck, split pickup and anodized guard — as being the most desirable on an early Precision.*

Fender Precision 1963 *(right) Later changes to the Precision included during 1959 the addition of a separate rosewood fingerboard to the instrument's customary maple neck. Earlier in the 1950s Fender had begun to offer colored-finish guitars. By the late 1950s they had standardized these options into a set of 'custom colors' which were based on the range of paints made for automobiles by DuPont. This attractive Precision is finished in Lake Placid Blue, a typical custom color of the early 1960s.*

James Jamerson *(above) Many of the classic Motown basslines of the 1960s were played by sessionman Jamerson, who used a 1962 Precision. His greatest lines, full of melodic invention and rhythmic surprise, include 'Reach Out' (The Four Tops) and 'You Keep Me Hanging On' (The Supremes).*

11

line of lap-steels and amps as he had with K&F, and soon moved production work into two steel buildings on nearby South Pomona Avenue. It was here that Leo survived near-crippling cashflow problems to come up with his Telecaster six-string solidbody electric guitar, and in October 1951 started producing the Fender Precision Bass. The company also added a good new bass amplifier to work with the instrument, the Bassman model.

Fender's Precision shared much of its construction with the Telecaster. It had a 20-fret maple neck bolted to a pale yellow-finished ash body that bore a black pickguard and finger-rest, a single-coil pickup, a chromed metal plate under a volume and tone control, and a chromed cover each for the bridge and for the pickup. The bridge had two saddles carrying two strings each, and the strings passed through the body, anchored at the rear (see picture page 10). It was typical of Fender's early products in that it had an austere simplicity and was geared to easy, piece-together construction. All the principal design elements were shown in Leo Fender's patent for "the ornamental design" of the Precision Bass, applied for in November 1952 and issued on March 24th 1953. The electric bass guitar had arrived ... although nobody took much notice at the time.

GUITARIST OR DOUBLE-BASSIST?

Today, some years after Leo Fender's death, it's impossible to know exactly his motivation for introducing the Precision Bass. Did he, for example, expect to sell the instrument to double-bass players, or to guitarists? Probably both, of course: "Anyone with the necessary $199.50," might well have been Leo's reply. Most people who were there at the time say that Leo first determined a need for such an instrument by talking to the guitarists who came and went at his Fullerton works. They had realized that playing more than one instrument increased their employment opportunities, but guitarists who tried the big double-bass generally found it hard to play.

Maybe the Precision's name was a come-on to those who considered the unfretted neck of the double-bass imprecise?

Don Randall, general manager of Radio & Television Equipment Co, Fender's distributor in the early-1950s, recalls the Precision name more as a typical concoction of Leo Fender's technically-oriented mind. Randall in fact named all the Fender products except the Precision, and remembers how that came about. "Leo and I had a discussion about the new bass and he's telling me how precision it was, how you could fret it right down to a hundredth of an inch. Now who puts their finger a hundredth of an inch this way or that on a bass string? But he was so possessed with the fact that this was the first time that the fret layout on a bass was so precise. He said to me, 'You know, it's so precise we ought to call it the precision bass.' Well, why not? So it became the Fender Precision Bass."

Many years after the event, Leo told Klaus Blasquiz: "When you're a guitar player and you play [double-bass] you have to listen to the pitch: ordinarily your ears are at the end of the bass, because it stands upright. You have difficulties hearing the pitch because the drums and the other parts of the orchestra are so loud ... So we made the Fender bass, and the guitar player didn't have to worry about the pitch when he played with other instruments."

Some of Fender's early promotional material seems to have been designed to remind double-bass players that they too could benefit from the new instrument. For example, the first US music trade press coverage of the Precision Bass, in the April 1952 issue of *The Music Trades* magazine, is headed "Fender Bass and Amplifier Replace Old Style in 1/6 Size". The report continues: "The Precision four-string bass is a considerable departure from the old style standard bass in that it is only one-sixth the standard size and is played in the same position as a guitar, supported from the neck ... The neck is slender and fretted, which enables considerable ease and comfort for the player."

The Music Trades continued its 1952 news item by quoting Don Randall: "A finger style of playing is used rather than the old style of slapping and jerking the strings, which was necessary with the older style instrument to obtain sufficient volume," said Randall. "This new instrument when used with the Bassman amplifier produces considerably more volume than a conventional string bass, and with a great deal less effort on the part of the player. Bass players will find that they are less tired after a night of playing this instrument than with the older type."

And speaking today, Don Randall remembers that guitarists were not the only group of musicians at whom the new Precision Bass was aimed. "The guitar players picked it up, of course, and many of them played bass and guitar, but most of the guys in the traveling bands playing the big bass – they had to have a moving van to take everything where they were gonna go! The Fender was a godsend to them; it wasn't so cumbersome as the big acoustic bass." The tuning of the Fender bass, E-A-D-G, was the same as the double-bass, an octave below the lower four strings of the guitar. This familiarity was designed to attract both sets of players.

A MODEL SCALE

A question we can't now ask Leo is why he chose the scale-length of 34in for his Precision – and Don Randall confirms that it is correct to call it *Leo's* Precision: "Yes indeed, it was Leo's baby. But it was an outgrowth of the input of many musicians, and of people in sales who saw the need for it."

The scale length is the distance from nut to bridge saddle (or, to be more precise, double the distance from nut to 12th fret) and therefore determines the sounding length of the string and its relative tension, tone and playability. The 34in scale-length of Fender's new electric bass guitar was some nine inches longer than that of most conventional six-string guitars, a requirement derived from the much deeper pitch of the instrument, and around eight inches shorter than the average scale-length of the double-bass.

George Fullerton worked for Leo with only a few breaks from early 1948 through to Fender's death in 1991. Fullerton told Willie Moseley about the original experiments to determine the scale length of the Precision: "We tried some shorter scales like 30in and 32in but they didn't seem to get the resonance we needed. We may even have tried something like a 36in scale,

but when we got to that length the distance between the frets was too wide to be practical for a player. In trying to get things right regarding sound reproduction, we even took gut strings off of upright basses and wrapped wire over the part of the string that would be vibrating over the pickup."

Randall concurs that trial and error were the major factors in determining the scale-length: "It didn't have any basis in science, that's for sure!" he laughs. "I think it just probably evolved from trying to see what was the most convenient scale to play." Randall also agrees about the lack of strings for the new instrument: "Yes, the big problem was getting strings, and we had to go through some rigmaroles to get them. Simply, they weren't being made. It was either Mapes or Squier who made the first proper ones for us."

The Precision's body design was new for Fender, with an extra cutaway on the upper horn when compared to the Telecaster, and it later inspired the body shape of Fender's Stratocaster guitar. Fullerton recalls: "For the Precision Bass we pretty much followed the Telecaster shape. The reason for the extra cutaway was the strap – because on the upper side you don't need a cutaway anyhow. This longer neck on the bass and the heavier keys made it overbalanced, and so by extending the top horn you put the suspension for the location of the strap holder more in the center, to offset the balance. All these things were designed into it for a particular reason, we wouldn't just say oh, I'm gonna put a horn on it. But in those days nothing was available, for instance there were no bass keys available. We used to take great big keys that fit on those hollow basses and cut them down, trim them to make them fit."

WAS LEO CRAZY?

In those years at the start of the 1950s few other guitar companies took seriously Fender's new direction with the electric bass. Forrest White, who worked as Fender's production chief from 1954, remembers a salesman telling him about the reaction to the Precision Bass at an early trade show: "Those who were not sure if Leo was crazy when he brought out the solidbody guitar were darn sure he was crazy now, since

13

Höfner 500/1 c1956 *(below)*
Höfner was established in Germany in the 1880s, and by the 1950s was making electric guitars and basses. The 500/1 is often called a 'violin bass'.

Gibson Electric Bass 1953
(left) This first Gibson bass guitar was firm evidence of the 50-year old company's traditional outlook. In an attempt to lure double-bass players to the new electric instrument, Gibson made their short-scale Bass in a down-sized double-bass shape (even painting on a fake f-hole). A telescopic spike was provided to enable it to be played upright (far left), while rear-facing 'banjo' tuners (above) helped to dispel any guitar associations. It was dropped by Gibson in 1958, soon after being renamed EB-1 to match the new EB-2.

Höfner *(above) Shown is a rare early 500/1 with oval control panel, and decal on the body rather than the headstock.*

Kay ad 1953 *(above) Kay were experienced makers of double-basses ('viols') and had offered a model named after Woody Herman's bassist Chubby Jackson in the late 1940s. Here Jackson demos Kay's $150 short-scale 'electronic' bass, an early addition to the bass guitar market in 1952.*

Hang-tag (left) A thumbs-up from McCartney must have worked wonders for Höfner's UK sales agent Selmer.

Höfner 500/1 c1962 (above) This German 'violin bass' belongs to Paul McCartney, and was the second Höfner that the Beatle acquired. McCartney bought his first, with 'close-together' pickups, in Hamburg around 1961. The left-handed Beatle received this one in 1963, and it was used on many Beatles recordings and concerts, including the group's last show in San Francisco in 1966, and for post-Beatles work like Paul's 1990 world tour.

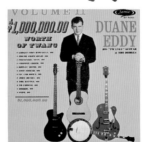

Rickenbacker 4000 1957 (above) Among the pioneers of the early electric guitar, Rickenbacker was established in California in the 1930s. This first-year example of their debut bass model bears the company's typical 'horseshoe' pickup on a body design that has survived for over 30 years. (See also 4001 p22/23 and 4001S p33.)

Duane Eddy (left) This 1962 album sleeve shows that Duane's essential arsenal included a Danelectro UB2 six-string bass, which he used for twangy low runs on hits like 'Because They're Young' (1960).

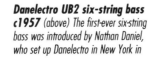

Danelectro UB2 six-string bass c1957 (above) The first-ever six-string bass was introduced by Nathan Daniel, who set up Danelectro in New York in 1955. Like most early six-strings, this was in effect a guitar tuned down an octave, at the time having more appeal to guitarists than bass players.

he came up with an electric bass. They were convinced that a person would have to be out of their mind to play that thing."

One exception was the Kay company of Chicago, best known for cheap and cheerful guitars and equally budget-conscious double-basses. With this particular combination of market interests, Kay in 1952 became the first to join Fender in adding a bass guitar model to their line. Kay advertised the K-162 'electronic' bass guitar in 1952 and were clearly trying to attract both double-bass players and guitarists. Woody Herman's bass player Chubby Jackson had been associated with Kay since 1945 when the company had issued a 'signature' double-bass, the S-51 Chubby Jackson five-string model, and he is pictured in the ad (see page 14) trying out the $150 short-scale bass guitar with a bemused grin. Kay pointed out in embarrassed tones that it looked like "the bass stance is a bit unfamiliar to Chubby".

The 1952 Kay ad continued: "It's held like a guitar, looks like a guitar… and is played like a guitar. BUT the pitch, range and tone quality are the same as a big bass viol. Easy to finger, easy to master, particularly for the guitar player. Actual bass pitch." The 'bass viol' was an antiquated term for double-bass, while 'bass pitch' confirmed an E-A-D-G tuning. (Incidentally, bassist Donald 'Duck' Dunn, who went on to fame with a Fender in Booker T & The MGs in the 1960s, started out in the 1950s with one of those early Kay bass guitars.)

A few more years into the 1950s Kay offered the K-160 bass guitar, this time with a strange D-G-B-E tuning, "the same as the first four strings of a Spanish guitar except one octave lower". This unusual concoction did not last, but it underlines the fact that makers were still not at all sure what an electric bass was, or what players should use it for. In short, there were no rules.

HAMP-LIFIED FIDDLE

It wasn't just guitar makers who were unsure about the viability of the new bass guitar in the early-1950s. Players too were suspicious of this weird new concoction. Some double-bass players figured that anything with frets was somehow

'cheating' and not worthy of their consideration. Guitarists also began to gain the impression that as the bass guitar had fewer strings it must therefore be an instrument for second-rate musicians. This was the beginning of a stigma that was to last for some time.

Among the earliest musicians to use the electric bass guitar in a popular setting was Roy Johnson of the Lionel Hampton Band, as revealed in the first important publicity for the Fender Precision Bass, less than nine months after its launch. The US jazz magazine *Down Beat* of July 30th 1952 featured a photograph of jazz vibraphonist and big-band leader Lionel Hampton posing with a Precision. Hampton's big band of the time combined swing and R&B in a sort of early form of jazz/rock'n'roll fusion, with an emphasis on crowd-pleasing solos, rhythmic grooves and a punctuating brass section. Clearly Hampton was open to new ideas and new ways of performing music – exactly the kind of broad-minded setting where the innovative electric bass guitar could flourish. In that issue of *Down Beat*, below the picture of Hamp and bass, was a report headed "Hamp-lified Fiddle May Lighten Bassists' Burdens" by noted jazz writer Leonard Feather (double-basses were sometimes referred to as 'bass fiddles'). Feather wrote of a bass revolution where players would no longer have to lug around a heavy, cumbersome instrument.

"It first became apparent some months ago when Lionel Hampton's band played a gig in [New York City]," Feather continued. "Suddenly we observed that there was something wrong with the band. It didn't have a bass player. And yet – we heard a bass. On second glance we noticed something even odder. There were two guitars – but we only heard one. And then the picture became clearer. Sitting next to the guitarist was someone who held what looked like a guitar at first glance, but on closer inspection revealed a long, fretted neck and a peculiarly shaped body, with electric controls and a wire running to a speaker. 'Sure man,' said Hamp excitedly when we asked him later, 'that's our electric bass. We've had it for months!' He introduced us to Roy Johnson, the Kansas City bassist who for all these months had been trudging around the country, unheralded, playing this sensational instrumental innovation. But Johnson has himself a whale of a plaything – a whale built like a sprat, to boot."

ELECTRIC MONK

Johnson faded from Hampton's band, but the electric Precision Bass stayed. Hamp's next bassman was William 'Monk' Montgomery (1921-1982), brother of guitarist Wes, whom Fender's Don Randall remembers very well. "Monk was the guy who really got us off the ground with our electric bass," he says, recalling that Fender used a drawing of Monk with Precision in their 1957/58 catalog (see page 3). Randall continues: "The Hampton band made a European tour and we got some glowing reports back from Monk, he would write me and say boy, it's going down well. In fact he was getting all the notoriety that Hampton should have got, because everybody was overwhelmed by this guy playing an electric bass. We got newspaper clippings from all over western Europe."

That tour started in September 1953 in Sweden, and Britain's *Melody Maker* headlined their report "Hampton Knocks 'em Out At Oslo Debut". Underneath was a prominent picture of Monk playing his Fender Precision Bass at the concert alongside the guitarist. The caption read "Not Two Guitars: The duettists are William Mackel on guitar with William Montgomery – on electric bass."

Nobody knew quite what to make of this weird new instrument, and as Hampton's European tour continued, more reports appeared. Ralph Berton wrote about the October 1953 Paris date for *Melody Maker*, and was clearly mystified when it came to Montgomery: "He produced some really inspiring sounds on an electrically amplified bass which resembled a large guitar." A month later *Melody Maker* decided in the wake of all the interest generated by Montgomery's bass guitar to see what British double-bass players thought of the new-fangled device. The reactions were unanimous: "Frankly, I don't see the point." "It looks nothing like a bass and can only sound like an electric guitar." "It can only be a weak note amplified." "It can never produce a perfect sound, all you get is an amplified

plink-plonk." And so on, confirming the horrified reaction.

But Montgomery got the last word. Tracked down at London Airport on a stopover on his way home to the US with the Hampton band, Montgomery was shown these criticisms by a brave *Melody Maker* journalist. Montgomery shrugged them off. "It's the greatest thing that happened," he told Mike Nevard. "I joined Hamp with an ordinary bass, but he liked the electric kind. His last bass man had one, he said I ought to get one. I didn't like the idea at all, but I got one. Boy was I glad! I had to start learning all over again, but there's nothing like it. The whole thing about it is that you get a better tone. And since our piano player left I've found even more advantages. For instance the electric model seems to fill in a lot for the missing piano, it gives a kind of depth to the rhythm that's missing when the piano's not there. I play a Fender: it's not a special job, a California firm turns it out."

INSTRUMENTAL BLEND

In an interview with Maggie Hawthorn in 1980, Montgomery told how Hampton had insisted that he play the electric bass the day he arrived to join the band. Montgomery objected, saying that no mention had been made of this when they'd talked before, and that he'd brought his double-bass to play. Montgomery recalled his meeting with Hampton: "He said, 'Then I'll just give you two weeks salary and your fare back home.' No way! I'd just left home, right?"

It's interesting to speculate why Hampton was so keen on the electric bass. Montgomery said that Hampton just liked the sound and volume of the instrument. "Because he could hear the bass, *really* hear the bass. When there's an upright bass in the band, you don't really hear it as much as you feel it ... the instrument blends into the music, it isn't dominant. Hamp used to come back to my amp and turn it up," continued Montgomery. "You know how Hamp would sort of prance or parade in front of the band. That happy sound, and he'd be sweating and the music getting to him ... and he'd clap his way over to the amp and turn it up because he wanted more bass, I guess. He liked that sound."

Gibson EB-2 1960 (above)
Gibson's previous basses had been solidbody models, but the EB-2 was launched in 1958 at the same time as the ES-335 guitar and shared its new 'semi-solid' construction. This involved a solid wooden block in the center of the EB-2's otherwise hollow body, effectively providing the tonal characteristics of both solid and hollow instruments in one bass. The hollow-body look of the EB-2 was a stylistic bonus for Gibson's ailing bass range at a time when Fender did not offer any hollow-body competition. (Note that the cherry finish of the example shown is unusual; most EB-2s came in natural or sunburst.)

Bill Wyman (right) The Rolling Stones' bassist bought his Framus Star Bass in 1963, around the time of the group's first single, to provide a harder sound than he'd been getting from his Vox. This British ad indicates that Wyman was still using the Framus in 1965.

Harmony H22 1963 (above)
During the 1960s Harmony of Chicago was the biggest US producer of guitars, and this bass is typical of their varied output. Steve Winwood's bassist brother Muff used one of these in The Spencer Davis Group in the mid-1960s.

Tuners (above right) Rear-facing Kluson types, often called 'banjo' tuners, were only seen on early versions of the EB-2, and were changed during 1960 to conventional side-facing units.

Epiphone Rivoli 1960 (above) The New York-based Epiphone company was bought by Gibson in 1957. One of the first so-called 'Gibson Epiphone' products was the Rivoli Bass of 1959, virtually identical to Gibson's EB-2. At first it was offered in natural or sunburst, later in cherry, and a two-pickup version was issued in 1970.

Epiphone catalog c1962 (left) The Rivoli proved especially popular with 1960s British bassists such as The Animals' Chas Chandler. This brochure from UK distributor Rosetti prices the bass at 162 guineas (about $260).

Framus Star Bass 5/150 c1962 (above) Framus was founded in 1946 in what was then the new West Germany, producing a range of musical instruments including violins and cellos. Guitars appeared in the 1950s, and the company's first electric basses, including the Atlantic model, were launched later in that decade. The Star Bass model followed, and at various stages was offered in different sizes and body styles. However, the type shown here featuring a large body with single cutaway and two pickups became best known thanks to its use in the 1960s by Stones man Bill Wyman.

19

Gradually more guitar makers began to produce bass guitar models. Gibson put out their Electric Bass toward the end of 1953 (the first model left the factory in September) with a solid mahogany violin-shaped body that seems to have been designed to appeal to double-bass players. Gibson had briefly ventured into violin and double-bass production in the late 1930s, although of course by the 1950s the company was much better known for guitars.

Gibson's short-scale Electric Bass had an optional 'spike' that fitted to the bottom of the body and allowed the bassist to play the instrument upright … like a double-bass. This apparently rarely-used facility was nonetheless provided well into the 1960s on various makers' basses, including Gretsch, indicating the continuing confusion over who would be playing the bass guitar.

INDULGING GUITARISTS

Ted McCarty, president of Gibson at the time, says they made the Electric Bass because their salesmen had received requests for such an instrument – presumably as a result of the Fender and Kay electric bass guitars already on the market. Gibson's 'violin' design was copied a few years later, albeit with a hollow body, by the German Höfner company. This probably would have failed to make the history books had not a young British musician named Paul McCartney taken up the Höfner in 1961 – of which more later.

Gibson added a few more short-scale bass guitars to their catalog later in the 1950s, including the EB-2 of 1958 which was a bass version of the company's new ES-335 guitar, sharing its new body design that placed hollow 'wings' around a solid central block, designed to offer hollow-body and solidbody tones in one instrument. At the same time Gibson renamed the violin-shaped Electric Bass the EB-1, but dropped that model in the following year, replacing it with the solidbody EB-0, effectively a bass version of Gibson's double-cutaway Les Paul Junior guitar. Gibson seemed to view their bass models merely as four-string versions of the more important guitar models, and the company indulged guitarists who wanted to play bass by offering bass guitars only with short 30½in scale-lengths.

DUANE & THE DANELECTROS

New Yorker Nathan Daniel produced his first Danelectro guitars around 1955, although his main business was building instruments under the Silvertone brand for the Sears Roebuck mail-order company. Daniel's instruments were boldly styled and, while cheap and using basic materials such as masonite, they worked surprisingly well. Around 1956 Danelectro produced the first six-string electric bass guitar, the UB2, effectively a guitar tuned an octave lower than usual. Like other early bass guitars from Kay and Gibson, the Dan'o had a short scale-length (29½in) – Fender was still the only maker offering a 'full' 34in-scale bass – but also featured a two-octave, 24-fret neck that was unusual for the time. Guitarists were the target for this instrument, evident from Danelectro's 1956 catalog that introduced the UB2: "A six-string guitar with extra-long neck and fingerboard, and extra-long strings."

Daniel recalls: "People started making bass guitars, and it was no big deal for us to switch from guitars to basses: we simply made the neck a bit longer. We started with a six-string bass because it's hardly any more trouble than a four-string and it gave the player something more for the same money. It took time for that to catch on, but if the player was capable, he had more stuff to play with." For a great example of Danelectro six-string bass on record, listen to Duane Eddy's 'Because They're Young' (recorded January 1960), or hop forward to Glen Campbell's 'Wichita Lineman' (1968). Session bassist Carol Kaye says she loaned Campbell her six-string Danelectro bass for the gorgeous solo. Kaye also played on Ritchie Valens' 1958 hit 'La Bamba' where it sounds suspiciously like a Dan'o six-string bass holding the chaos together.

Other companies added six-string basses to their line: Gibson in 1959 with the hollow-body EB-6, and Fender in 1961 with the solid Bass VI. But these were still essentially 'baritone guitars', normal six-string guitars down an octave, and were principally aimed at guitar players. None was especially successful, although the Danelectro was popular in a specialist studio role (see page 24), and British bassist Jack Bruce would briefly use a Fender Bass VI in his early Cream days in the 1960s before moving to a Gibson EB-3.

Danelectro went on to add a very distinctive bass to their catalog around 1958, the 24-fret Long Horn model, available in four- and six-string versions, followed by a more conservative Short Horn bass with just 15 frets in 1959. Nathan Daniel explains the outrageous look of the Long Horn bass (see page 25/26) as purely practical: "The idea was simply to give the player as much access as possible, which meant instead of a single cutaway, we had a deep cutaway on both sides. It did make an unusual look, sure, but it was an unusual name too: a couple of long horns," he laughs.

Some years later John Entwistle tried to use a Danelectro for his bass solo on The Who's 1965 single, 'My Generation'. "So as to get the right effect, I had to buy a Danelectro bass, because it has thin little strings that produce a very twangy sound," Entwistle told Dave Marsh. But the strings broke easily and, as no replacements were available in London, he simply went and bought two more Dan'o basses after breaking strings during the recording of early takes. Eventually he gave up, and the final version that is heard on the record was made with a Jazz Bass — strung, rather surprisingly given the resulting sound, with LaBella flatwound strings. Entwistle went on in the 1960s to pioneer the new 'roundwound' strings from British company Rotosound. Bass guitarists could then choose between the traditional tones of the established flatwound strings or the bright, bell-like sound of the new roundwounds.

ROGER ROSSMEISL'S RICKENBACKERS

The Rickenbacker company of California had been an early yet frustrated pioneer in the electric upright bass field. In 1953 founder Adolph Rickenbacker sold his company to Francis Hall, whose Radio & Television Equipment Co distributed Fender's early products. Hall's business relationship with Fender ended soon after he bought Rickenbacker, and Hall set about modernizing and revamping the Rickenbacker product

line, principally through the efforts of German-born guitar maker Roger Rossmeisl who joined the Californian outfit early in 1954. The company's first bass guitar, the 4000 model, is a typically unusual Rossmeisl design bearing a large body with angular horns. It was the earliest electric bass guitar to feature a scale length (33½in) virtually the same as Fender's 34in Precision, and the 4000 first appeared on Rickenbacker's July 1957 pricelist at $279.50 ($60 more than a Precision).

The Rickenbacker 4000 is also historically interesting as the first bass guitar to be constructed in the 'through-neck' style: the neck is not bolted (like Fender) or glued (like Gibson) to the body, but extends right through the length of the instrument, with 'wings' attached either side to complete the full body shape. A purported benefit of such a design is that the strings and their associated bridge, nut and tuners are all located on the same piece of wood, enhancing sustain and tonal resonance. More likely Rickenbacker found this an efficient and straightforward production technique; Rossmeisl had already tried it out for the company's innovative Combo 400 guitar of the previous year.

The general design and through-neck construction of the 4000 was used by Rickenbacker for many of their other bass models in years to come, including the fancier two-pickup 4001 (introduced 1961) and the export version with dot markers, the 4001S. Rickenbacker also offered on some models an unusual pseudo-stereo option, 'Rick-O-Sound', which separated the output of the two pickups so that a special split cord would feed the individual signals to two amplifiers (or to two channels of one amplifier).

ROCK'N'ROLL GOES ELECTRIC

Despite additions to the bass guitar market in the mid 1950s by makers competing with Fender's Precision, popular use of the electric bass guitar remained scarce at this time. The emerging rock'n'roll music stayed for the present in the hands of double-bass players: Al Rex with Bill Haley's Comets ('Rock Around The Clock' hit number one in the US in May 1955), Bill Black with Elvis Presley ('Heartbreak Hotel' 1956) and Joe B Maudlin

Gibson catalog 1962 (right)
Gibson's bass line also included the
single-pickup EB-O model at this
time, as shown in British distributor
Selmer's brochure. The EB-O had
changed to the 'SG'-style body
shape in 1961.

Rickenbacker 4001 1964 (above) After their early single-pickup 4000 bass (see p15), Rickenbacker added a two-pickup version, the 4001, in 1961. The new 4001 also featured distinctive checkered body binding and triangular-shaped fingerboard markers.

Fender Bass VI 1962 (above) From its vibrato to the tight string-spacing, this 'baritone guitar' was clearly aimed at guitarists rather than bass players. It offered guitarists a bass sound by being tuned one octave below a normal guitar. This one is the early three-switch version.

Gretsch 6070 1963 (below) Gretsch's hollow-body models succeeded their earliest bass, the solidbody Bikini of 1961. But the company never did well with basses, not least because few famous players used them. The 6070 had a body spike so that it could be played upright.

23

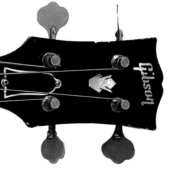

Gibson EB-3 1962 (above) Like the majority of Gibson's basses of this period the EB-3 had a short-scale neck which, together with its humbucking pickups, contributes to the EB-3's deep, muddy tone. Short-scale basses have proved much less popular than the standard long-scale instruments.

Jack Bruce (right) The best known player of the EB-3, Bruce adopted Gibson's distinctive sounding bass while a member of Cream in the 1960s.

with Buddy Holly's Crickets ('That'll Be The Day' 1957). Bill Black got a Fender Precision around 1957: photographs reveal one in the MGM studio during the filming of *Jailhouse Rock*, and Presley's title track recorded in April sounds as if it features Black on Fender.

By 1957 Fender basses were being seen more frequently on stage – contemporary photos reveal a Precision in the live bands of Jerry Lee Lewis and BB King, among others. Around the same time the bass guitar began to infiltrate American studios, too. Duane Eddy's instrumental hit 'Rebel Rouser', recorded in March 1958, featured two bass players: Jimmy Simmons plays double-bass to give depth and tone to the bassline while Buddy Wheeler plays the same notes on electric bass guitar, adding a percussive, attacking edge – what Eddy's producer Lee Hazelwood called 'click bass'. This technique turns up on other records made around this time, notably in Nashville where it was termed 'tic tac bass', for example Presley's 'Stuck On You' (March 1960) with Bob Moore on double-bass and session guitarist Hank Garland on six-string electric bass, Patsy Cline's 'I Fall To Pieces' (November 1960) with the tireless Bob Moore on double-bass and Harold Bradley on Danelectro six-string bass, or German easy-listening king Burt Kaempfert's many hits which began with the November 1960 single 'Wunderland Bei Nacht'.

Guybo Smith added a trebly bass guitar contribution to Eddie Cochran's 'Summertime Blues' hit of August 1958, while in the UK Brian Gregg created a pleasing throb below Johnny Kidd & The Pirates' raucous 'Shakin All Over' (1960), and a rash of instrumental pop tunes began to feature players like Nokie Edwards (on The Ventures 'Walk – Don't Run', 1960) and Jet Harris (on The Shadows 'Apache', also 1960) who underlined the bass guitar's role as the natural partner to the lead and rhythm guitars in these new pop groups.

SNUBBING THE TONE

But why did it take so long for the bass guitar to become established? The instrument's originator, Fender, made changes to the design of their Precision Bass in 1954 and 1957,

indicating that they were still searching for a combination of features that would attract musicians. The final alterations of 1957 – new pickup, larger headstock, different pickguard – defined the look of the Precision Bass for decades to come.

Don Randall recalls that one of the reasons for enlarging the headstock concerned a shortcoming of the Precision Bass design. "We had a problem with a deadspot on the first string, around the seventh fret. A lot of people never found that out," he laughs, "but some of the better bass players did. We worked to try to overcome that, and enlarging the headstock helped some. I think we determined that the resonance of the body, neck and head with the seventh fret position acted like a shock absorber, it kind of snubbed the tone. The mass of the body and of the head and the stiffness of the neck all had an effect on the problem, but we never did solve it completely."

Despite the slowly growing awareness of bass guitars among players, all the signs are that guitar companies still regarded the electric bass with caution at the start of the 1960s. Harmony, a very big Chicago-based musical instrument company, were not at all slow in identifying and exploiting market opportunities … and they did not offer a bass guitar until about 1962, with the launch of their H22 model. Similarly, Fender had not felt that the market would support a second model in their bass line until 1960, in stark contrast to the rest of their growing product lines of the time which included six distinct electric guitar models and no less than 13 different amplifier heads and combos.

GETTING INTO JAZZ

The new Fender was the Jazz Bass, which the factory started to produce in March 1960. It first appeared on the July pricelist at $279.50 in sunburst or $293.47 in blond or custom color (the Precision Bass was shown on the same list at $229.50 sunburst, $240.97 blond/custom color). "We were always market driven," explains Fender's Don Randall. "After establishing the fact that bass guitars would sell and that people wanted them, then the next thing was to make a prettier one, a more elaborate one. We wanted an upscale model to put on the

Gibson flyer 1964 (above) A rare example of Gibson publicity putting the bass player up-front. Nonetheless, it's emphasized that the "ultra-modern shape" of the Thunderbird bass is "made to match the Firebird guitar"

Gibson Thunderbird IV 1964
(left) This bass belongs to John Entwistle and was The Who bassist's main stage and studio instrument from 1972 to 1976 (when he changed the original control knobs). The Thunderbird was Gibson's most stylish bass, launched in 1963 and sharing the 'reverse' body shape and through-neck construction of Gibson's new Firebird guitar. The two-pickup Thunderbird iV was partnered by a single-pickup model II. The T'Bird has been regularly reissued, and is especially popular today with metal bands.

Gibson Thunderbird II c1968
(left) Gibson decided to revamp the design of the Thunderbirds in 1965 after poor sales, and complaints from Fender about similarities to their guitars. Ironically, the new style was more Fender-like, exaggerating the offset-waist style but with a more conventional 'non-reverse' shape. Construction was also changed, from the through-neck style to Gibson's more usual glued-in neck joint. But the new look did little to boost the T'bird's popularity at the time, and this version was dropped in 1969.

26

Vox Stinger IV 1967 (right) This pear-shaped body style made the UK-built Vox instruments instantly recognizable, not least when used by players like The Rolling Stones' Bill Wyman. The Stinger model was part of the later Italian-made Vox line, but retains the 'teardrop' body, very thin neck and odd, oversized headstock.

Body (below) The Jazz Bass has an offset-waist body shape, similar to that of Fender's Jazzmaster guitar which the company had introduced in 1958, two years before the Jazz Bass.

DUAL PICKUPS

NARROW NECK

ADJUSTABLE BRIDGE

TRUSS-ROD REINFORCED NECK

COMFORT CONTOURED BODY

Fender features (right) Taken from a 1965 Fender catalog, these drawings show hallmarks of the Jazz Bass such as its offset body shape, narrow nut and twin pickups.

Fender Jazz Bass 1960 (above) The Jazz Bass featured two new pickups that resulted in a wider tonal range than that of the earlier Precision. The narrower neck also provided players with a different feel. At first the Jazz Bass was fitted with two 'dual-concentric' volume/tone controls (often called 'stack-knobs'), as on this launch-year example which is also desirable thanks to its 'custom color' finish, this one officially known as Olympic White.

Poster (right) Bassist Marcus Miller, best known for his work with jazz trumpeter Miles Davis on albums such as 'Tutu' (1986) and 'Amandla' (1989), has for many years used a Fender Jazz Bass (pictured far right). This announcement for a concert given by Miller in London in 1994 highlights his association with the Fender instrument.

Fingerboard (below) Early Jazz Basses came with rosewood fingerboards, at first in 'slab' style (with a straight join between neck and fingerboard), changing in 1962 to a 'veneer' style (with a curved join), and bound from the mid-1960s.

IN CONCERT
MARCUS MILLER
JAZZ BASS
c.Marshall Arts Ltd presentation

Labatt's ★ APOLLO
HAMMERSMITH
SATURDAY 2nd JULY
Tickets £17.50* & £16.00*
CREDITCARD
BOOKINGS
071 416 6090
jazz fm
102-2

Neck (above) This is narrower at the nut than the Precision Bass, providing a relatively tight string spacing.

Burns Bison Bass 1962
(below) The British maker's eccentric bass package included three pickups, distinctive horns (appropriate for a Bison), and four controls, which included a pickup selector labeled Tenor, Treble, Bass and — an absolute essential — Wild Dog. The standard black finish lends the bass its customary 'Black Bison' nickname.

FAMOUS LONG HORN BASS
an original design by DANELECTRO

FEATURED BY LEADING RECORDING STARS

Danelectro Long Horn Bass c1961 (below) US maker Nathan Daniel produced his first Danelectro bass in 1956, the six-string UB2 (see p15). Next in line was this unusual Long Horn model, rather optimistically advertised in the early 1960s (left) as the bass used by "leading recording stars". However, despite the cheap materials — masonite bodies, for example — they work surprisingly well, delivering a crisp, cutting tone.

Finish (left) The Long Horn came in this bronze sunburst, or 'white sunburst'. The tuners (far right) are not original.

Fender Jazz Bass 1977 (below)
This is Marcus Miller's bass, modified
for him by guitar maker Roger
Sadowsky. Maple fingerboards with
black markers were offered as an option
on the Jazz from the late 1960s.

Headstock (above) This gold
'transitional' Fender logo preceded the
black company logo of the late 1960s.

Jaco Pastorius (right) Among the
most highly rated players to use the
Fender Jazz was Jaco Pastorius (1951-
1987). Early in his career he had
removed the frets from his main
instrument to create a fretless bass.
During the 1970s Pastorius defined the
fretless sound, both on-stage and on
records such as his solo album 'Jaco
Pastorius' (1976), Joni Mitchell's
'Hejira' (1976) and Weather Report's
'Heavy Weather' (1977). Drug-related
problems culminated in Jaco's tragically
early death after a bar brawl.

Fender Jazz Bass 1964 (above)
This example is owned by Guy Pratt
who used it on the 1987 and 1994
Pink Floyd world tours, as well as for
many other sessions and concerts. This
beautiful Fender custom color is called
Burgundy Mist, and the instrument has
the standard three-control set-up used
on all but the earliest of Jazz Basses.
Pratt has substituted the original Fender
pickups with 'active' replacements
(these by EMG), a popular move
among bassists seeking a more modern
tone than the 1960s pickups can offer.

market. The Jazz Bass wasn't Leo's idea particularly, it was more of a marketing idea, something that we wanted to expand the line. Mostly it was not just a love of the product, it was a market oriented move."

The design of the Jazz Bass was distinguished by its offset-waist body, similar in style to the Jazzmaster guitar that Fender had launched two years earlier. The Jazz Bass also differed from the Precision in its narrow string spacing at the nut, which gave the neck a distinctly tapered feel, and its provision of two pickups which offered wider tonal variation. Fender's Precision Bass always outsold the more expensive Jazz Bass: some players preferred the out-and-out simplicity of the Precision; others opted for the crisper tones and the different feel of the Jazz.

The pickups of the Jazz Bass were linked in humbucking mode, as was the 'split' pickup of the Precision that had been used on the redesigned Precision since 1957. Leo Fender later explained to several interviewers that in the 1950s Fender never emphasized the humbucking capabilities of their pickups because their patent attorney had told them that this type of pickup had been patented back in the 1930s.

FENDER HUMBUCKERS

Leo also said that humbuckers were introduced on the basses because he considered the earlier single-coil type of pickup too hard on the amplifier's loudspeakers, whereas the humbucking types offered a softer, less spiky signal, no doubt easing the Fender amp repair department's workload. Leo's patent for the Precision 'split' pickup (filed January 1959 and issued March 28th 1961) puts it in more detail: "Electric guitars of the bass type have, in recent years, been coming into use as a replacement for the very large and clumsy string basses conventionally employed. Such bass guitars are sufficiently small to be held on the lap of a seated guitarist, and require relatively little transportation and storage space. Furthermore, such guitars are much simpler and less strenuous to play than conventional non-electric string basses," reads the Fender document.

The pickup patent continues: "In order to achieve the necessary low pitch, the guitar strings must be much more bulky and massive than those of a standard guitar. Furthermore, the excursion of each string on both sides of the neutral position, resulting from each plucking or picking action, is greater than that of a string of a standard guitar. These and other factors have made it exceedingly difficult to provide an electro-magnetic pickup construction which will properly convert the string vibration into electrical impulses, and which may be adequately adjusted to the various strings in order to achieve the desired volume relationships." Fender's 'split' humbucking pickup did much to solve these problems: the position of the pickup units relative to the strings was fully adjustable; electrical interference hum was canceled; and string vibration was more accurately sensed.

BEATLE BASS

Pop music exploded in popularity as the 1960s got underway, and demand for electric basses boomed because the bass guitar finally became accepted as an integral part of the studio and stage lineups of the new pop groups. Nobody did more to fuel this demand than The Beatles, who from 1964 became, quite simply, the most popular and visible group in the world. They had self-contained playing and composing skills, and also established the required quartet personnel of two guitars, bass guitar and drums. Paul McCartney, born in Liverpool in 1942, started out as a guitarist, but became The Beatles' bassman when their first bassist decided he was a better artist than a musician and would leave the group.

McCartney explains: "Stu Sutcliffe was a friend of John Lennon's, they were at art school together, and Stu had won a painting competition. The prize was $120. We said to him, that's exactly the price of a Höfner bass! He said it's supposed to be for painting materials, but we managed to persuade him over a cappuccino. It kind of dwarfed him a bit, the [large-body] Höfner, he was a smallish guy, but it looked kind of heroic. He stood a certain way, he had shades, he looked the part … but he wasn't that good a player, he hadn't played anything up to buying that bass. Stu was suddenly there just because he could afford it. None of us wanted to be the bass player, it wasn't the number one job: we wanted to be up front. In our minds it was the fat guy in the group nearly always played the bass, and he stood at the back. None of us wanted that, we wanted to be up front singing, looking good, to pull the birds."

The Beatles had landed a second grueling season of gigs in Hamburg, Germany, in mid-1961. "Stu had said he was gonna stay in Hamburg, he'd met a girl and was going to stay there with her and paint. So it was like oh-oh, we haven't got a bass player. And everyone sort of turned round and looked at me. I was a bit lumbered with it, really, it was like well … it'd better be you, then. I don't think you would have caught John doing it, he would have said: 'No, you're kidding, I've got a nice new Rickenbacker!' I didn't have a guitar at the time – it had been smashed up and I was playing piano on stage then – so I couldn't really say that I wanted to be a guitarist. So … eventually I found a little shop in the center of Hamburg, and I saw this violin shaped bass guitar in the window, the Höfner."

It was a Höfner 500/1 model, a German-made hollow-body similar to Gibson's Electric Bass, and generally referred to as the 'violin bass'. McCartney, a left-hander, acquired his first Höfner in 1961, and recalls buying for the equivalent of about $45 a right-handed model which he turned upside down (although all the photographic evidence of the band in those early years implies that he actually started with a production left-hander). McCartney had a number of different versions of the Höfner 500/1 over the years, but stuck to the model as his sole Beatles live performance bass, and as the principal bass for the group's recordings until later in the 1960s.

JAMERSON GEMS

On the other side of the Atlantic a player from a different background was also beginning to make a mark. James Jamerson was born in South Carolina in 1936, and moved with his family to Detroit, Michigan, in 1951. At the age of 18 Jamerson started to play double-bass, with jazz ambitions, but in 1959 began to play sessions for a record company in Detroit

owned by Berry Gordy. The company would soon be known throughout the world as Motown. With remarkable foresight Gordy christened his company of black musicians 'The Sound of Young America'. Motown's fresh merger of pop and R&B from artists such as The Supremes, The Four Tops, Smokey Robinson, Marvin Gaye and Stevie Wonder became just that, attracting a huge audience of both black and white fans during the company's heyday from 1964 to 1967.

Jamerson switched to electric bass in 1961, buying a Fender Precision when Gordy asked him to go on the road with Jackie Wilson. After a few changes brought about by theft, Jamerson settled on a 1962 sunburst Precision. In 1964 Gordy moved Jamerson from road duties to become a full-time member of Motown's fluctuating team of studio musicians, unofficially known as the Funk Brothers. Jamerson shines out on Motown hits like The Supremes' 'Stop In The Name Of Love' (1965), The Four Tops' 'Reach Out' (1966), and Stevie Wonder's 'I Was Made To Love Her' (1967), among many others. His powerfully rhythmic basslines were often beautifully melodic, and his recorded work with Motown helped to change the perception of the electric bass guitar's role in pop music from root-note machine to an important part of the overall musical picture.

Back in England in the early-1960s Paul McCartney was one of many bass players who heard Jamerson's arresting basslines and noted the magical sound and musical invention. Not that anybody knew that it was James Jamerson they were hearing. Session players were not credited on Motown records (nor on many others in those days). "As time went on," recalls McCartney, "James Jamerson became my hero, although I didn't actually know his name until quite recently. Jamerson and later Brian Wilson of the Beach Boys were my two biggest influences: James because he was so good and melodic, and Brian because he went to very unusual places."

McCartney himself was hardly inhabiting everyday bass worlds as the 1960s progressed. Gradually his basslines became more melodic and were pushed further forward in the Beatles mix. He'd been given a Rickenbacker 4001S (see page 33) on The Beatles' August 1965 US tour and started using it in the

Fender Bass V c1966 (right) The
first five-string bass, the Bass V adds a
high C-string above the usual E-A-D-G.
While retaining the full 34in scale, the
Bass V featured a short 15-fret neck,
with the fifth string catering for the
upper registers. The theory was that
bassists, particularly readers, could play
with greater ease in positions 'across'
the strings rather than 'along' the
fingerboard. However, players did not
agree, and the Bass V was shortlived.

Ampeg AEB-1 c1966 (right) Everett
Hull formed the Ampeg company in New
York in the late 1940s to make
amplifiers and pickups for double-basses.
In the early 1960s the company
produced an electric 'upright' bass, the
Baby model, followed in 1966 by the
first fretless electric bass guitar, the AUB-
1. The example shown is the otherwise
identical fretted version. Its early
transducer-style pickup (termed the
'mystery pickup' by Ampeg) is hidden
from view under the bridge, and the f-
holes pass right through the body,
creating a very distinctive and unusual
styling. For a number of years the
influential AUB-1 was the only available
purpose-built fretless bass guitar.

Ampeg headstock (above)
Looking like the peghead of a
double-bass, Ampeg's 'scroll' head
was intended to emphasize to
double-bass players the similarities
between this bass and their
customary instruments. Ampeg
used the 'scroll' head on the
AUB/AEB-1, as well as on the
peculiar ASB-1 bass (see inside
front flap of jacket).

Fender catalog c1967
(above) Note that this Bass V
still has its pickup cover and F-
for-Fender bridge cover. Players
often found that these chrome
'ash-trays' got in their way, and
usually removed them.

Boz Burrell (right) Bassist with King
Crimson (1970-72) and Bad Company
(from 1973) Burrell is seen here in
concert with Bad Company playing an
Ampeg AUB-1 fretless, which he used
extensively on the band's early records.
Other prominent players of Ampeg's
unusual 'scroll' basses are rare,
although Rick Danko of The Band also
used a fretless model to good effect.

Guild Starfire Bass I

1967 (left) The Guild company started making the hollow-body Starfire range in the 1960s. The best known user of the bass was Jack Casady (above) of San Francisco band Jefferson Airplane. His two-pickup Starfire II was heavily modified by Alembic, an electronics outfit also based in San Francisco that went on to great fame as a bass maker.

Chris Squire (above) Playing with British progressive band Yes in the early 1970s, Squire produced a distinctively bright, driving sound from his 4001S that did much to popularize the Rickenbacker bass models at this time.

33

Horn (left) This has been slightly reshaped by owner Paul McCartney.

Body (left) Originally 'fireglo' red, Paul McCartney's Rickenbacker 4001S bass is now down to a natural wood finish.

Rickenbacker 4001S 1964 (right)

This bass belongs to Paul McCartney, and was given to him by Rickenbacker on a Beatles' American tour in the mid-1960s. McCartney used it on many Beatles records from 1965 onwards, and it can be seen with a suitably psychedelic refinish in the 'Magical Mystery Tour' movie. McCartney also used this Rickenbacker on Wings tours and recording sessions. The 4001S was an export version of the 4001 (see p22/23) made primarily for the UK. The main distinction of the 4001S, now highly collectible, is the unbound fingerboard with dot inlays.

studio during October and November to record songs for the group's *Rubber Soul* album. From that point on he would alternate between the Rickenbacker and his trusty Höfner, although by the time he got to record the superb 'lead-bass' parts for the *Sgt Pepper* album at the end of 1966 and into 1967 he was using the Rickenbacker as his main studio instrument.

McCartney remembers that he started to experiment with basslines, moving away from the simpler efforts of earlier recordings based on the root notes of chord sequences. "I wondered: what else could you do, how much further could you take it? *Sgt Pepper* ended up being my strongest thing on bass, the independent melodies. On 'Lucy In The Sky With Diamonds', for example, you could easily have had root notes, whereas I was running an independent melody through it, and that became my thing. So once I got over the fact that I was lumbered with bass, I did get quite proud to be a bass player. It was all very exciting."

LESH, ENTWISTLE, CASADY & BRUCE

By 1964, well over ten years after Fender's Precision had first appeared, the electric bass was at last becoming established as *the* modern bass instrument. In their different ways, McCartney and Jamerson personified this new acceptance. McCartney was an unschooled pop musician, originally a guitarist who was 'lumbered' with the bass, but who made the instrument his own and showed it off to the world. Jamerson came from a jazz background playing double-bass, but found pop studio work with an electric bass more lucrative, and soon discovered that he could make wonderfully expressive music on bass guitar, proving to many session players that the electric bass was a legitimate musical instrument.

Improvements to stage and studio equipment during the 1960s made the bass guitar increasingly audible, and vital musical steps were taken by players such as Jack Bruce in Cream, Phil Lesh in the Grateful Dead, John Entwistle in The Who and Jack Casady in Jefferson Airplane, along with studio bassists like Tommy Cogbill (Wilson Pickett, Aretha Franklin, Percy Sledge), Carol Kaye (Beach Boys, Glen Campbell,

Monkees), Joe Osborn (Simon & Garfunkel, Mamas & The Papas, Fifth Dimension) and John Paul Jones (Dusty Springfield, Herman's Hermits, Donovan) among many others.

Guitar makers too were reacting to the changing musical atmosphere around the bass guitar in the 1960s, although some still viewed the instrument as a kind of lesser version of the guitar. Fender, however, were on a roll, and in the mid 1960s 'Fender Bass' became a generic expression, synonymous with electric bass guitar. In the 1965 American Federation of Musicians' directory of union members in Local 47 (Los Angeles), for example, there were three headings for bass guitarists: 'Electric Bass', 'Bass Guitar', and 'Fender Bass'. The 'Fender Bass' listing was the longest, and included active LA session musicians like Carol Kaye and Ray Pohlman.

In January 1965 Fender was sold to CBS (Columbia Broadcasting System) for $13 million and became the Fender Musical Instruments division of Columbia Records Distribution Corporation. CBS poured millions of dollars more into Fender and increased its output dramatically, but as a result quality gradually declined into the 1970s and the original team that had built up Fender grew disenchanted and one by one left the new organization.

THUNDERBIRD TOO

The Precision and Jazz were still superb Fender mainstays, but the new models that did show up – an unusual 15-fret five-string with extra high C-string, the Bass V (1965), Fender's first short-scale bass, the Mustang (1966), and a reissue of the original-style Precision as the Telecaster Bass (1968) – all did little to expand or enhance Fender's catalog beyond the company's leading bass duo.

Gibson for their part had modified their bass line in 1961 to include the new EB-0 and EB-3 solidbody basses, and in 1963 and 1964, clearly with an eye on Fender's growing bass success, issued two Thunderbird models, Gibson's first long-scale bass guitars. (They appeared on Gibson's July 1963 pricelist at $260 for the single-pickup II and $335 for the two-pickup IV. As a comparison, Fender's basic price at this time

34

for the Precision was $229.50 and for the Jazz Bass $279.50.)

As well as their long scale, Gibson's Thunderbird basses were also a departure for the company in that they used through-neck construction and featured fully adjustable bridges. Maybe they were too radical, however, and sales were poor. A revised Thunderbird design appeared in 1966, after Fender complained of infringements to its patented offset-waist body design, but Gibson was still relatively unsuccessful with bass guitars.

FRETLESS, F-HOLES, DEVIL HORNS

In 1966 Ampeg launched the first fretless bass guitar, the AUB-1. Ampeg had been set up in New York in the late 1940s by two double-bass players, Everett Hull and Jess Oliver, to market a bass pickup system (see page 8) and (in the early 1950s) bass amplifiers, the latter still highly regarded today by electric bassists with an ear for quality sound.

Dennis Kager, a guitarist and electronics engineer, had in 1964 joined the company, now based in New Jersey, and at first his job was to check and adjust the Burns guitars and bass guitars that Ampeg were importing from the UK. Ampeg had been making an electric mini double-bass since 1962, the Baby Bass, having acquired the design from the Dopyera Brothers, best known for their Dobro resonator guitars, who had sold the bass under the Zorko brand. Ampeg improved it and Jess Oliver came up with a new diaphragm-style pickup, which the company cleverly called 'the mystery pickup', a term coined by Ampeg's sales manager Jim Tite.

"Bass was the love of the old man," says Kager, referring to Ampeg boss Everett Hull, who was over 60 years old in 1965. "Everything was directed at bass. A lot of the professionals playing in New York City would come in, and some would say, 'Gee, you guys ought to make a Fender bass.' They would say that they'd lost jobs because the studio wanted a Fender bass and they only played double-bass. So we went ahead and started making prototypes of a bass guitar in 1966. We knew how to make the necks because we made the Baby Bass, but we had to come up with a hip body. So they said to me,

design a body for us." Kager did not have to search too widely. He was playing Fender Jazzmaster and Stratocaster guitars at the time, so he came up with a body shape that mixed the two: the offset waist of the Jazzmaster with the rounded base of the Strat. But his imagination took a leap when he added two f-holes that went right through the body. "I don't know where that came from," he laughs, "but I thought the top hole could work as a handle to carry the bass."

Kager approached the design of the bass from a guitarist's point of view: he wanted a Fender-style headstock shaped like an A for Ampeg, and a magnetic pickup, also like Fender's. Hull on the other hand was more inclined to offer a guitar which would appeal to double-bass players as an extra instrument that would help them get work in the newly popular role of bass guitarist. And so the prototypes began to acquire the 'scrolled' double-bass headstock and diaphragm under-bridge pickup, both features borrowed from the Baby Bass.

The idea of a fretless fingerboard also came from Hull and Oliver. "The double-bass players would take the fretted bass guitar, what we called the horizontal bass, and complain that the fingering was different." explains Kager. "The fretless bass guitar was a way of allowing the double-bass player to comfortably get into the horizontal bass without so much trouble as the fretted version."

Two models went into production in late 1966, the fretted AEB-1 (Ampeg Electric Bass) and the fretless AUB-1 (Ampeg Unfretted Bass). Ampeg also tried out around this time a body design put forward by another employee, Mike Roman, but his bizarre Longhorn-style Ampeg bass – "the ugliest thing I've ever seen," says Kager, "looked like devil horns on it" – was short-lived and few were made (see picture on inside front jacket flap). The f-hole-body Ampeg basses sold reasonably well, although they remained as something of a local specialty, and naturally could not compete with Fender's market dominance. But as the first commercially available fretless model, the AUB-1 was a significant development. Fender themselves did not offer a fretless bass until their Fretless Precision model of 1970.

35

Gibson Les Paul Bass c1970 (left)
This shortlived bass was derived from the
Les Paul Professional guitar. It was
quickly replaced by the Triumph Bass,
itself a bass version of the Les Paul
Recording. Like many guitar makers,
Gibson tended simply to adapt existing
guitar models into basses, despite
declaring itself 'The Bass Place' (below).

Hagstrom H8 c1967 (right) Among
the first production eight-string basses,
the H8 was built by Swedish company
Hagstrom. The strings are arranged in
four pairs, the second of each pitched an
octave above the 'normal' string.

Fender Precision fretless c1973
(above) It took Fender until the early
1970s to produce a fretless version
of their industry-standard Precision
model, despite a growing
interest among players in the
unique sound offered by fretless
basses. Although it is possible to
approximate the sound of a
double-bass with a fretless
instrument, it does have a
beautiful voice of its own, quite
distinct from the fretted bass.

Ampeg catalog c1970 (above) Starting out as a guitar repairer in New York, Dan Armstrong was invited by Ampeg to help with the design of an acoustic guitar. Armstrong suggested a plastic electric guitar and bass, and he is pictured in this Ampeg brochure playing his perspex-bodied instrument.

Ampeg Dan Armstrong 1970 (right) Ampeg were once again involved with a new development, making the first solid perspex bass in 1970 (built some ten years earlier than Steinberger's more celebrated use of man-made materials). Dan Armstrong (see above) decided to carve bodies from blocks of clear perspex, simply to make the resulting short-scale bass look different than anything else available. In this he certainly succeeded, but the bass lasted little more than a year in production, hindered by conservative players and an expensive manufacturing process.

Fender Mustang c1969 (right) After Fender were taken over by CBS in 1965 the company's marketing strategy changed. The Mustang, offered from 1966, was their first short-scale bass, aimed to be more accessible for the new generation of guitarists now also playing bass. This is the custom-colored 'competition stripe' version.

Gretsch catalog 1968 (above) The short-scale bass was a popular compromise in the 1960s, as some makers thought of basses merely as alternative instruments for guitarists.

Other experiments were being undertaken by guitar companies keen to squeeze more sales from the newly discovered bass guitar market. Ampeg later teamed up with New York guitar repairer Dan Armstrong to produce a distinctive acrylic-bodied 'see-through' bass, while in Sweden the Hagstrom company came up with one of the first eight-string bass guitars, the H8, in 1967. This followed the pattern adopted by 12-string guitars of using paired courses of strings, with one string of each pair an octave higher than the 'normal' string. A few contemporary records featured the ringing sound of the H8, such as Jimi Hendrix's 'Spanish Castle Magic' (recorded October 1967, played by Noel Redding) and Richard Harris's 'MacArthur Park' (1968, Joe Osborn).

Some makers' experiments of the late 1960s were geared to expanding the simple electronics used so far in bass guitars. Burns in Britain had been the first to incorporate 'active' electronics into a bass: their semi-solid TR2 model of 1963 featured an on-board battery-powered pre-amplifier that enabled the player to boost treble and bass tones (normal 'passive' circuits can only cut from existing tones).

Gibson issued their Les Paul Bass in 1969 with low impedance pickups, designed to offer greater tonal character and quieter operation when connected to low impedance equipment such as some recording gear. However, the Les Paul Bass was supplied with a special cord that had a built-in impedance-matching transformer to boost the output from the low impedance pickups to a level suitable for use with normal (high impedance) instrument amplifiers. By 1971 the Les Paul Bass had been renamed the Les Paul Triumph Bass, and redesigned with a built-in matching transformer and a different control layout. In general, bass players ignored these apparently complicated basses produced by the Gibson company which appeared to have been designed with recording engineers rather than musicians in mind.

DEADBEAT

A more significant development of bass guitar electronics was going on at the same time in a setup that was about as far removed from the orthodox business environment of a big-league guitar organization like Gibson as it was possible to get. Alembic started out as one observer put it "as more of a concept and a place than a company". The place was San Francisco, the time was 1969, and the motivating force was one Augustus Stanley Owsley. His main source of income was from the manufacture of (then legal) LSD, a good deal of which seems to have been consumed by the premier psychedelic group of the time, The Grateful Dead. Part of the community of roadies, friends and acid freaks that gradually grew up around the Dead was a sort of electronics workshop known as Alembic, named after an apparatus used by distillers (and also apparently by alchemists) "to convey the refined product to a receiver", as the dictionary defines it.

Owsley had created Alembic in the warehouse where The Grateful Dead rehearsed in Novato, California, about 30 miles north of San Francisco. At first the idea was for Alembic to come up with new ways of providing clear, accurate recordings of Dead concerts so that the band could improve their live performances. This developed into a general interest in the improvement of studio and live sound quality, primarily by examining and refining all the different elements of the musical process, from instruments and microphones through to the PA systems and recording equipment that come at the end of the musical chain.

ALEMBIC SOUND WIZARDS

Alembic quickly branched out into three main areas, becoming a recording studio, a developer of PA systems, and a guitar repair/modification workshop. The combination of the woodworking talents of Rick Turner, a one-time Massachusetts folk guitarist and guitar repairer, and the electronics knowledge of Ron Wickersham, who came to Alembic from the Ampex recording equipment company, soon turned the workshop into a full-fledged guitar making operation. Alembic became a corporation in 1970 with three equal shareholders: Rick Turner, Ron Wickersham and recording engineer Bob Matthews.

"We started to customize instruments," explains Turner, "what we called 'Alembicizing'. Some Guild Starfire hollow-body basses were Alembicized for Phil Lesh of the Dead and Jack Casady of Jefferson Airplane in 1970 and 1971." The very first official Alembic instrument made to the new company's own design was a bass guitar built for Jack Casady in 1971 (see picture page 40/41).

By 1973 the Alembic recording studio in San Francisco was becoming a financial headache, but in September of that year a savior appeared in the shape of a two-page article about Alembic, "Sound Wizards to The Grateful Dead", in *Rolling Stone* magazine. Turner says: "The article was seen by the guys at L D Heater, an instrument distribution company based near Portland, Oregon, owned by Norlin. They had been given a mandate by Norlin to go find some new manufacturers' product to distribute, so they came to us and said, 'What would you do if we gave you a purchase order for 50 instruments?' At that point I think we'd built only 32, but it looked like rescue from bankruptcy to us. So we went to the bank and got enough for me to go and consider how to tool up the Alembic factory."

HIPPIES AND CASHFLOW

In that *Rolling Stone* feature from summer 1973 Charles Perry described the young Alembic team as "the Grateful Dead family's coven of hi-fi wizards", and quoted them as "aiming for that thing electronic music has, its ability to transcend technology". Turner was Perry's guide through the Alembic workplaces: he explained to the *Rolling Stone* writer how he had combined his own-design pickups with Ron Wickersham's electronic systems, showed Perry yet another bass being built for the Dead's Phil Lesh, demonstrated the sophisticated controls of a typical Alembic bass, and described the Dead's Alembic PA system.

"All our experimentation is aimed at giving the musician as much control as possible," Turner said, and photos accompanying the *Rolling Stone* piece showed the company's two main premises: the workshop at Cotati, about 40 miles north of San Francisco, where Alembic's woodwork, metalwork

and pickups were made principally by Turner and Frank Fuller; and the Alembic office in nearby Sebastopol where Wickersham dealt with electronics production. The image propounded by the *Rolling Stone* feature was of amiable, talented hippies who rolled with the flow and did their best to indulge the 'straights' of the business world.

"There seemed to be enough cashflow happening by this point and we had a fairly star-studded clientele, to the point where we got away with it," laughs Turner in reflective mood. "We started to slowly standardize a regular line of short-scale, medium-scale and long-scale basses, at first based on the Guild Starfire Bass, and with equivalents in guitars – although at that point we probably made 19 basses or more to every guitar. Bass players were far more interested in a new, clear approach, whereas guitar players seemed satisfied with what they had. Guitar players appear to be inherently more conservative than bass players when it comes to equipment."

MYRTLE MEETS VERMILION

Alembic's unique alliance of design elements had been relatively quickly established. The instruments featured a high quality multi-laminate neck-through-body construction, attractive, exotic woods, heavy, tone-enhancing brass hardware and complex active electronic systems with external power supplies. "The laminate necks and, for example, the overlay on the back of the pegheads really came out of my love for old banjos," explains Turner. "Many of the really high-end banjos from the 1910s and 1920s often featured laminated necks of contrasting wood stripes. I liked the aesthetic, and it made sense to me structurally as well. As for the neck-through-body, it was frankly a much easier way to put together a nearly hand-made instrument than figuring out how to make a really accurate joint and glue it.

"We felt that we were getting our tone from the solid, rigid neck-through, and that what we then put on the wings of the instrument was far less important … in fact Heater, our distributor, never knew what we were going to send them, there was no standard wood selection for an Alembic. I'd go buying

Body (below) The unusual 'rails', allowing pickups to slide into different positions, did not become a standard feature of Alembic's future models.

Alembic #001 1971 (above) This is Alembic's very first bass, built for Jefferson Airplane bassist Jack Casady. It marks the beginning of a line of instruments that significantly influenced bass making, with their striking use of exotic woods, sophisticated active electronics, multi-laminate through-necks, and the sheer quality of their construction. (The original electronics of this bass have been modified.)

Stanley Clarke (above) One of the best-known Alembic players, Clarke pioneered fusion bass-playing, with Chick Corea in Return To Forever (1972) and on solo albums from 1974.

Fingerboard *(below)* To counter bad attacks of stagefright, the names of the notes are inlaid between the frets.

Alembic 'Spider' 1981 *(above)* John Entwistle had Alembic make him three of these custom basses, celebrating his classic Who song 'Boris The Spider' by featuring a spider's web made from silver wire inlaid into the body wood.

Fingerboard *(above)* The custom 'tree-of-life' uses silver and pearl inlay.

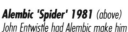

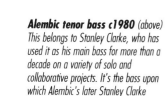

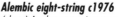

Logo *(right)* Alembic was set up in 1969, at first to fulfill the eccentric requirements of San Francisco groups such as the Grateful Dead and Jefferson Airplane.

Alembic eight-string c1976 *(above)* Another custom instrument, this one was built for ELP bassist Greg Lake and currently resides at the Hard Rock Cafe in London. It should be noted that in addition to their custom work Alembic offer many standard models.

Alembic tenor bass c1980 *(above)* This belongs to Stanley Clarke, who has used it as his main bass for more than a decade on a variety of solo and collaborative projects. It's the bass upon which Alembic's later Stanley Clarke Signature series was modeled. Clarke's distinctive 'lead-bass' sound derived from the use of higher-pitched tunings, most often his octave-higher 'piccolo' style or the 'tenor' tone that resulted from the A-D-G-C tuning of this bass.

wood, and what I saw and what I liked I'd get, whether it was California walnut, or myrtle, or zebrawood, padauk, vermilion, cocobolo, whatever. The wood selection was whatever we happened to want to do that day or week or month. And I think Heater turned it to advantage: it was the craftsman's inspiration as to what the woods were going to be, and no two were alike. That became a selling point in itself."

Wickersham describes his experiments with the Alembic bass's active electronics as primarily an attempt to get more high frequencies from the instrument without having to boost the signal at the amplifier. "The pickups in those days had very high inductances," he says, "and we found that even going through a short run of cable reduced a lot of top-end response from them. So we had to mount the active circuit directly into the bass."

STAN THE MAN

By this time bassist Stanley Clarke had bought his first Alembic instrument, after Turner had taken an Alembic bass to a Return To Forever gig in San Francisco and invited Clarke, who at the time used a Gibson EB-2, to try it. Clarke later recalled for Tom Mulhern: "He told me in a nice way, 'Look, you really play well, but your sound is atrocious.' So I tried it out and it was great... I didn't know what any of it meant, but it sounded *the end*. And that night on the gig it was like a new bass player had been born. I could suddenly play anything that I heard in my head."

Stanley Clarke was born in Philadelphia in 1951, and first played accordion, quickly moving to violin, cello and double-bass, and switching to electric bass for high-school bands. His first gigs included work with jazzmen such as Stan Getz, Dexter Gordon and Horace Silver. In the 1970s Clarke came to personify the new breed of bass player, elevating the bass guitar to the role of soloing instrument and equal partner to the other frontline instruments. Clarke had joined Return to Forever with keyboard player Chick Corea in 1972, and the group forged a highly successful fusion of jazz, rock and Latin flavors in the early-1970s. Clarke's first solo album to feature prominent electric bass appeared in 1974, the first of a long line, and these

more than any other records established the idea that a virtuoso bass guitarist could become a star.

Ron Wickersham remembers the effect of Clarke's use of Alembic basses at the time: "The year the *Rolling Stone* article came out, 1973, was the year that Stanley Clarke bought his instrument, and then people around the world seemed to learn more about him than of our local San Francisco musicians. So he *propelled* us. There was a combination of Stanley whose star was rising very fast promoting us to other high-end musicians, and our new distributor, L D Heater, promoting us to the music stores and educating the salesmen in those stores. All of a sudden we were pretty well known pretty fast."

With all Alembic's deluxe features and monied clients and one-of-a-kind sales talk — even blinking LED lights up the fingerboard if you wanted — the basses were, as you might expect, very expensive. An L D Heater brochure from around 1975 shows an Alembic bass pegged at $1250. The most expensive new Fender would have cost about $430 at that time. Bass players were clearly becoming more willing to accept new ideas and designs than guitarists, and some bassists were beginning to pay for the privilege. Thanks to Alembic the specialist, high quality, high price bass guitar had arrived.

GRAPHITE YARN

Before Turner left Alembic in 1978 the company encouraged some experiments with a new material generally referred to as graphite. A more accurate term than 'graphite' would be 'reinforced plastic', a composite material made from fiber and resin. Carbon, glass or graphite fiber, which usually comes as a continuous yarn or 'weave', is saturated with a liquid resin and molded to produce a thermoset object. The result is not only denser and stiffer than wood, but a great deal stronger and much lighter than steel, with greater resistance to extreme temperatures and stress. It was these qualities that attracted Alembic and led them to make some experimental bass necks from graphite. "We had realized at that point that stiffer was better in a neck," says Turner, "at least in terms of evenness of tone and lack of deadspots." These 'deadspots' are areas on the fingerboard where the note does not ring as clearly or sustain for as long as the other notes when sounded. This has proved a notoriously frustrating problem for both maker and player alike when dealing with wooden-necked instruments in particular, which rarely manage to avoid deadspots.

Geoff Gould was working for an aerospace company in Palo Alto, just south of San Francisco, and was familiar with the graphite material being used for some of the company's satellite parts that required light weight coupled with strength and stability. In 1974 Gould, a bass player himself, went to a Grateful Dead concert and took a good look at Phil Lesh's Alembicized bass. Assuming it to be a heavy instrument because of all the controls and electronics added on, Gould started to wonder whether a bass made from graphite might be a good idea. He took some graphite samples to Alembic, and it was decided to try to make some hollow graphite short-scale bass necks.

At first the graphite neck idea was offered as a potential production item to Gould's aerospace employers, who were apparently keen to diversify into consumer products, but they declined. Following that, an Alembic bass with one of the experimental graphite necks was exhibited at an American musical instrument trade show in 1977, and a patent filed just under a year later. Straight after the trade show John McVie of Fleetwood Mac bought that bass, the first ever to employ graphite technology.

WOOD'S LOW-KEY RIVAL

Gould formed Modulus Graphite with other ex-aerospace partners in order to make graphite necks for Alembic among others, and later produced their own replacement necks and graphite-neck instruments. Turner's name appeared on the graphite-neck patent as inventor, and the patent was assigned to Modulus Graphite. Turner left Alembic in 1978 and started Turner Guitars, steering away from basses and toward guitars. Modulus also made graphite necks for Music Man (see page 64) for their Cutlass bass model, and Turner sold his share of the patent to Music Man around 1980. Music Man folded and

the rights to the graphite neck reverted to Modulus. This new material for bass guitar necks had thus been established as a serious if low-key rival to wood, and it was used intermittently by Alembic and various other makers. Alembic continued as a prestigious high-end bass specialist, adding new models to their Series I and Series II basses as the years progressed. Meanwhile over in New York, and quite independently, some rather more spectacular applications of graphite were about to take place – and this time the result would be a bass guitar molded entirely from the material.

THE STEINBERGER REDESIGN

Ned Steinberger moved to New York in the 1970s after graduating from art school, and started working as a cabinet maker and furniture designer. He soon moved into a space at the Brooklyn Woodworkers Co-operative, another member of which was guitar maker Stuart Spector. Steinberger began to take an interest in Spector's work, and discovered that Spector was trying to develop a new bass guitar design.

Stuart Spector had become interested in guitar building when he had made an instrument for himself, and in the early-1970s went on to build guitars and a few SB bass models, the latter being through-neck basses of conventional shape that sold mainly in the New York area. Spector began to think about a bass design that would have more impact … and by coincidence along came Steinberger.

"At the time I barely knew the difference between a bass and a guitar, let alone between different brands," laughs Steinberger. "It was easy to learn what the different elements of a bass are and, coming from furniture, my main focus was to work up some ideas towards making a more comfortable instrument," Steinberger explains.

"I'm a designer – not a furniture designer or a guitar designer, but a *designer*. Once you understand how things are made you can learn about and design all kinds of things. I didn't think that I would become so heavily involved in the music business – at the time it was a bit of a one-shot deal in my mind: design an instrument. But I think that what drew me

43

Body (below) Echoes of the NS bass turn up in later designs by Warwick, Tune and other makers.

Spector NS2 c1985 (above) Ned Steinberger's first bass design appeared in 1977, produced as the one-pickup NS1 by New York maker Stuart Spector, who soon added the two-pickup NS2. The body design, with its comfortable 'curved' cross-section (see back view in the NS1 catalog, right), proved popular with many US players. The Kramer company bought Spector in 1985, continuing to 1990; by 1993 Stuart Spector was back in business.

Kramer 650B c1977 (right) Gary Kramer, previously a partner of Travis Bean (far right), set up his own operation to exploit aluminum necks, producing a wide variety of models from 1976 based on wood/aluminum combination necks. But metal still felt strange to some players, and by 1985 the company had rejected aluminum, opting for traditional materials.

DiMarzio ad 1980 (left) A fad for 'hot' replacement pickups grew in the 1970s, with DiMarzio (seen here on a BC Rich bass) the most popular.

BC Rich Bich c1985 (above) US maker Bernardo Rico's outlandishly shaped guitars first appeared in 1971. This one was built for Michael Anthony of Van Halen (note 'MA' first-fret inlay).

Earthwood Bass 1973 (below) Recalling the large Mexican guitarrón, the enormous Earthwood was produced by the Ernie Ball company in California in the 1970s – well before 'Unplugged'. This example belongs to John Entwistle.

Travis Bean TB2000 c1976 (below) Travis Bean and Gary Kramer initiated the use of aluminum necks with this Californian bass in 1974, but production lasted for only five years.

John Entwistle (above) The Who bassist is seen playing his Earthwood acoustic bass (pictured above left), clearly indicating its massive size. Not surprisingly, the Earthwood did not catch on, and more practically proportioned acoustic basses from makers such as Guild followed.

into instruments was the challenge and excitement of making such a special kind of product."

Steinberger began to suggest ideas and offer help to Spector. Vinnie Fodera, a fledgling bass guitar maker who started working for Spector early in 1977, remembers watching the beginnings of what became a Steinberger/Spector bass guitar design. "Ned was designing chairs and so on, he had an adjoining space to us in the co-op. It was a large open loft space, 5000 square feet, with numerous craftsmen sharing the area and chipping in for the rent. Ned displayed a talent for coming up with unique and artistic designs. He was looking at what we were making, casually, and I'm sure, because this is the way his mind works, he would get ideas when he saw what we were doing. We had a common lunch table, so at any time everyone might be sitting together having a sandwich or a snack – and we'd converse about our general problems and design ideas in our spare time."

ERGONOMICS

Steinberger's first consideration had been the overall construction and ease of production of the proposed bass. "I developed a system for assembling the body on a neck blank cut all the way from one end to the other along the line of the outside edge of the fingerboard," says Steinberger. "I hadn't seen that before and it doesn't seem to be done very much still, but that's the way the NS is made. And it's significant because that same cut goes all the way through the peghead, and then the two sides of the peghead are glued on. It makes a very simple and very strong kind of structure, which also is producible," he explains.

"Starting from that core, I glued the body parts on at an angle to that neck blank such that I was able to put a nice curve into the top of the body and also carve the back of the body to fit the player's mid section. I combined a nice arch on the top of the instrument primarily for a visual effect with another on the back primarily for comfort and playability."

The ergonomic Spector/Steinberger bass was launched in 1977 as the Spector NS-1 (the 'NS' standing for Ned

Steinberger), and as the 1980s got underway it influenced a number of other makers who noticed that it balanced well and was extremely comfortable to wear and play. Spector later introduced a two-pickup version, the NS-2, and production of the NS models continued after Spector was bought out by Kramer at the end of 1985. Kramer continued production until early 1991, when the company folded, and Stuart Spector is now back in business with new models based on the NS design.

OFF WITH ITS HEAD

Back in the late 1970s, Ned Steinberger had obviously been bitten by the guitar bug and began to formulate ideas for a further bass guitar design. This one would have far-reaching consequences and would, almost literally, turn many other makers on their heads. One of the things that Steinberger had had trouble with while working on the NS design was his uneasiness with the weight of the neck and tuning machines in relation to the body – and in fact to counteract this he had ended up adding some weight to the back of the early Spector NS bodies. "And that," says Steinberger, "is what led me to think about taking the tuning machines off the peghead and putting them on to the body."

He wasn't the first to think of this option, but nobody had made anything approaching a commercial impact with such a layout. "I made my first headless bass probably somewhere in 1978," says Steinberger. "I made it from wood, and it was really a disaster. I had this idea that I could make a lightweight and flexible instrument, and that if I isolated the vibrating system I would have the sustain and the kind of tone that I wanted. Well, after building this lightweight, flexible instrument I realized that I was just way off the mark. I almost gave up at that point. But I was challenged by that failure. I think that's what drove me forward, trying to understand where my thinking went wrong," he says.

That led Steinberger to consider the opposite of his first attempt: why not make the bass heavier and rigid? He had already noted 'deadspots', another drawback of existing bass guitars: although most notes sustain well, certain notes die

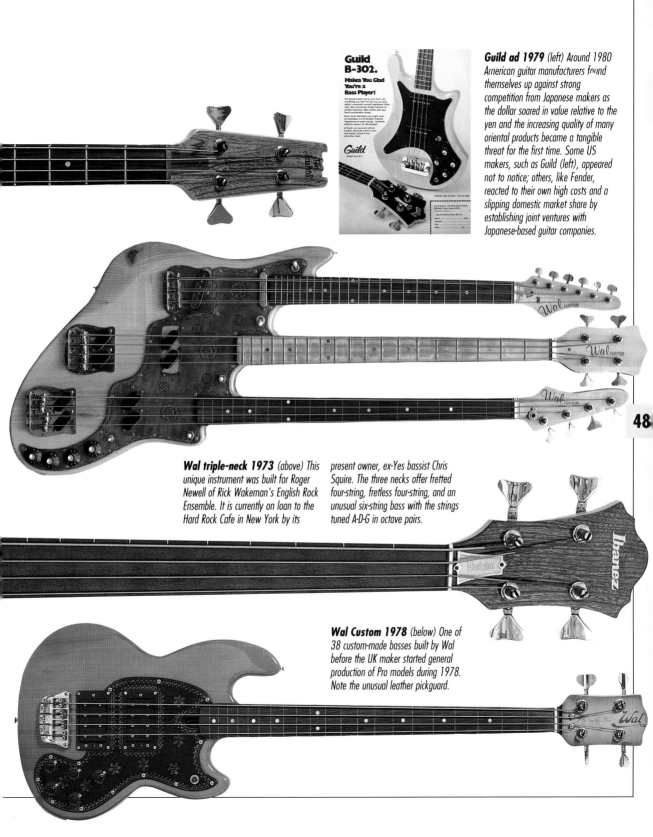

Guild ad 1979 (left) Around 1980 American guitar manufacturers found themselves up against strong competition from Japanese makers as the dollar soared in value relative to the yen and the increasing quality of many oriental products became a tangible threat for the first time. Some US makers, such as Guild (left), appeared not to notice; others, like Fender, reacted to their own high costs and a slipping domestic market share by establishing joint ventures with Japanese-based guitar companies.

Guild B-302.
Makes You Glad You're a Bass Player!

Wal triple-neck 1973 (above) This unique instrument was built for Roger Newell of Rick Wakeman's English Rock Ensemble. It is currently on loan to the Hard Rock Cafe in New York by its present owner, ex-Yes bassist Chris Squire. The three necks offer fretted four-string, fretless four-string, and an unusual six-string bass with the strings tuned A-D-G in octave pairs.

Wal Custom 1978 (below) One of 38 custom-made basses built by Wal before the UK maker started general production of Pro models during 1978. Note the unusual leather pickguard.

48

Music Man StingRay Bass 1979
(below) This is Pino Palladino's
StingRay, the bass on which he recorded
'Wherever I Lay My Hat' with Paul
Young in 1983 and defined the sound
of fretless bass in pop. It has been
Palladino's main bass on a multitude of
sessions, including work with Don
Henley and Elton John. Music Man was
started by ex-Fender employees Forrest
White and Tom Walker in 1972, joined
in 1975 by Leo Fender in order to add
basses and guitars to their amplifier line.
Leo's StingRay attempted to improve on
his earlier work, with a new headstock
layout and active electronics.

Logo (above) Music Man's two
guitarists are seen on all the company's
basses, guitars and amplifiers.

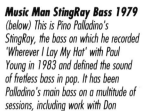

Controls (left) This set-up offers bass,
treble and volume; later an optional
extra mid tone control was offered.

G&L L2000 1987 (right) Formed in California in 1980, G&L originally stood for the forenames of the company's two founders, ex-Fender man George Fullerton, and Leo Fender. Fullerton sold out to Leo in 1986. The G&L basses never achieved the popularity of the Music Man instruments, but not surprisingly they continued to build on typical Fender features and principles. Earlier models can be identified by controls mounted on a Music Man-style chrome plate; later, the plate was omitted, as on the late 1980s two-pickup L2000 model shown here. G&L was sold to a new owner, BBE Sound Inc, after Leo Fender's death in March 1991.

Leo Fender (right) The predominance of basses here highlights Leo's post-Fender success with four-string models. Leo was in his seventies when this promotional photo was taken; as you might expect, the boss claims in the ad that G&L basses and guitars are "the best instruments I have ever made".

Music Man ads (left) Music Man's bass guitars became Leo Fender's second success story. Players like Tony Levin (far left) and many others discovered that Leo Fender had in effect updated his Precision, and ensured a lasting place in the bass establishment for the company's StingRay model. Complicated business maneuvers led Leo Fender to leave Music Man in 1980 and set up G&L, and a few years later the surviving Music Man people teamed up with the Ernie Ball string company, who continue the successful production of Music Man instruments.

Aria SB1000 1980 (below)
Introduced in the late 1970s, the
SB1000 gave new credibility to the
work of Japanese manufacturers. Its
through-neck construction and active
electronics are hallmarks of the period.

Sting (left) Sting's melodic,
constructive bass work was an
underrated component of The Police
(1977-83), from 'Can't Stand Losing
You' to 'Every Little Thing She Does Is
Magic'. While he has also used Fender
basses to good effect, especially for
subsequent solo material, Sting's most
prominent instrument in The Police was
his Ibanez Musician bass, shown in
concert (left) and pictured below.

Ibanez Musician 1979 (above)
This bass belonged to Sting
who used it for most of his
Police work. Ibanez, along
with Aria, redefined the
image of Japanese basses in
the late 1970s as well-made
and good sounding instruments,
bringing many features of expensive
custom makers like Alembic to a more
affordable line of basses.

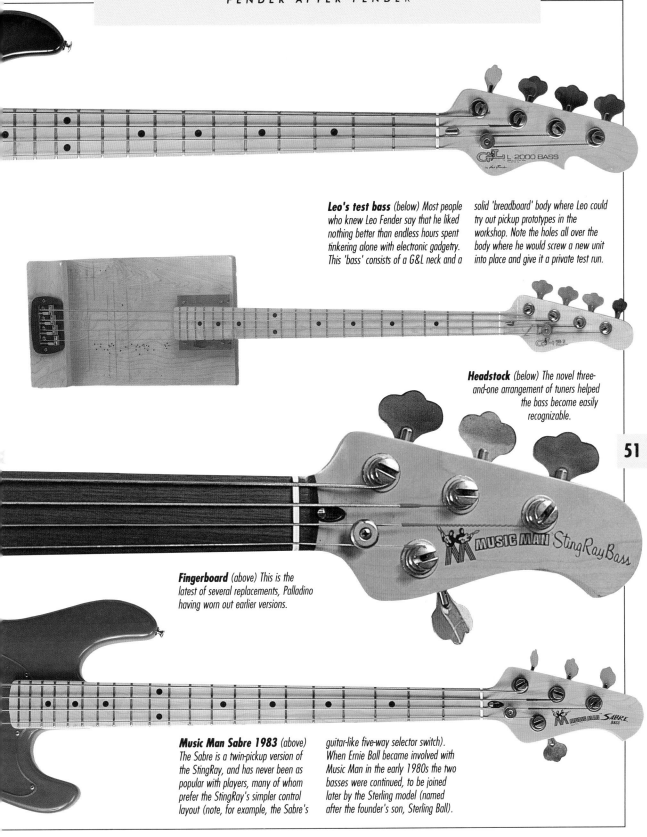

Leo's test bass (below) Most people who knew Leo Fender say that he liked nothing better than endless hours spent tinkering alone with electronic gadgetry. This 'bass' consists of a G&L neck and a solid 'breadboard' body where Leo could try out pickup prototypes in the workshop. Note the holes all over the body where he would screw a new unit into place and give it a private test run.

Headstock (below) The novel three-and-one arrangement of tuners helped the bass become easily recognizable.

51

Fingerboard (above) This is the latest of several replacements, Palladino having worn out earlier versions.

Music Man Sabre 1983 (above) The Sabre is a twin-pickup version of the StingRay, and has never been as popular with players, many of whom prefer the StingRay's simpler control layout (note, for example, the Sabre's guitar-like five-way selector switch). When Ernie Ball became involved with Music Man in the early 1980s the two basses were continued, to be joined later by the Sterling model (named after the founder's son, Sterling Ball).

quickly, primarily because of sympathetic vibration in the long, thin wooden neck. So he then clamped down his wooden prototype on to a heavy, rigid workbench, and was pleased to get the tone and consistent sustain he was looking for. Steinberger removed the bass from the workbench and sheathed it in stiff fiberglass, a material he'd worked with before in furniture making and boat building, and found tone and sustain still improved. He was on the right track.

"I did other experimentation and realized that the optimum material would be graphite," says Steinberger. "It's a reinforced plastic, a composite material mixing fiber and resin. It's a very rigid material that is a lot like wood: it's fibrous, and its specific gravity is not that much different. Resin is like sap in wood, if you will: that's what bonds all the fiber together. But the actual fiber in wood is made from the molecules growing end on end, it's directional. So the wood fiber is comparable to the graphite fiber, and the epoxy resin is along the lines of a glue that holds it together. Graphite is like a superwood, that's how I've always seen it."

STEINBERGER SOUND

Obviously the next move was to make a proper bass out of graphite. "I remember getting the graphite in and learning how to deal with it," recalls Steinberger, "and it was all rather difficult and full of setbacks, including having everything in my trial mold trashed with absolutely nothing to show for months of work."

Vinnie Fodera, still working with Stuart Spector, recalls Ned conducting many experiments around 1978 in the co-op loft, prior to actually building a bass. "He would purchase graphite cloth and he used to get epoxy by the gallon, he made molds and would concoct beams and put strings across them to see if they were more rigid than wooden beams," remembers Fodera. "He was constantly asking our opinions because he didn't understand all the musical qualities at that point, he was concerned more with the structural qualities of the synthetic material. It was very stimulating to be in that environment then, it was all new and experimental, and certainly Ned

influenced us as we influenced him. It was a feedback loop, and marvelous to be there."

Eventually Steinberger produced his first all-graphite bass. "I believe it was the first solid graphite instrument molded from head to toe," he says. "I don't know of any other instrument like that that has been made." Steinberger first showed the bass in public at a US trade show in 1979. It had all the attributes of the final Steinberger Bass: all-graphite construction, tiny rectangular 'body' with tuners on the end, headless neck, and active pickups. Initially, Steinberger's intention was to sell the design to one of the big guitar companies — he saw himself as a designer, remember, not as a guitar builder.

"In the furniture business, that's how it works, independent designers are commonplace," he says. "But in the guitar business it's just not the same." He approached Fender, Gibson and one or two others, but had no response. The only hint of curiosity came from Music Man, but that faded quickly. Steinberger says that he was especially disappointed by the lack of response from Kaman, a manufacturer famous for their Ovation plastic-backed guitars. After these thwarted attempts at selling the design, Steinberger decided to make the bass himself, and formed the Steinberger Sound Corporation in Brooklyn in December 1980 with three partners: Bob Young (a plastics engineer), and Hap Kuffner and Stan Jay (both of Mandolin Brothers, a Staten Island-based guitar dealer). The new operation launched their Steinberger Bass at the two big musical instrument shows of 1981 in Frankfurt, Germany, and Chicago, US, and while many industry people remained skeptical, some musicians warmed to the unusual new bass.

RADICAL DESIGN

Ned sold his first Steinberger bass, a fretless model, to session bassist Tony Levin, best known then for his work with Paul Simon and King Crimson. Steinberger says: "One of the guys who really did us the most good at the start was Andy West of The Dregs. I remember when he played for us at our first music trade show, he stepped up there with his new Steinberger Bass and just played his ass off. I learned a lesson there. We had been getting almost no interest at the show, and then the night before the last day of the show Andy got up there and played for the people, and the next day our booth was mobbed! So musicians helped us enormously."

The bass won some prestigious design awards, and magazine reviews praised the strange but effective new instrument: "the future of electric bass guitar"; "no self-respecting pro can afford to be without one"; "the best electronic bass I've ever played"; "the perfect bass for me"; "an exciting new chapter in the ongoing development of guitar construction"; "in a sonic category of its own"; and so on.

Several other notable and conspicuous players soon took up the Steinberger Bass, including Sting (Police), Geddy Lee (Rush) and Bill Wyman (Rolling Stones), and Steinberger Sound found that they had a success on their hands. At first they could only make around six basses a month, but by summer 1982 demand exceeded production capacity by 300 per cent, and toward the end of 1983 they were producing as many as 60 instruments a month. Steinberger recalls: "I think that a key reason why we were able to succeed with this strange headless design made out of plastic was that although at first glance it seemed very strange to a musician, on a second glance it starts to make sense, right on the surface. There's a certain logic in the instrument that is visible, that is understandable, that is communicable to bass players. That in my mind is one of the main reasons why we were able to pull off such a radical design."

Steinberger also notes that bass players are more interested in custom-made instruments than guitarists. "They're not so satisfied with their instruments," he says, "they're not so well established, and there's more interest in alternative bass guitars. Also, I think guitar players like to have a lot of different guitars, and don't necessarily want to spend all that much money on them, whereas a bass player's more likely to have just one or two instruments and put everything he's got into those," suggests Steinberger.

The design was enormously influential in the early-1980s.

One could almost imagine guitar factory workers from New York to Tokyo wielding their power saws and creating headless 'designs' overnight. Naturally Steinberger was not the first guitar making company to have their designs copied. Bass designs had long been copied – especially, though hardly exclusively, by oriental companies. But this was almost an epidemic. The Steinberger copying was not so much in the use of graphite, the expense and complexity of which put off most mass-market manufacturers, but more so in the small body and headless elements of the design, the immediate visual characteristics. The new buzzword among electric bass and guitar makers became 'headless'. Active pickups, supplied to Steinberger by California company EMG, also became very widely used on other instruments.

FROM GENESIS TO TRANSPOSITION

"The copying was an uncomfortable situation," Steinberger recalls. "But with all this copying going on a lot of people, including us, began to presume that everyone would be playing a headless guitar in ten years or so. Of course that turned out not to be the case at all, primarily because of the lack of acceptance of the visual style. But at that time everybody started copying the design, and a very important decision we made was to try to license the design rather than get into a lot of lawsuits. I don't think we would have survived otherwise."

Later in the 1980s, in conjunction with Genesis bassist Mike Rutherford and British guitar maker Roger Giffin, Steinberger produced their M series basses and guitars, with a more conventionally styled wooden body bolted to a graphite neck. A variation on the graphite neck concept with a headless through-neck and wooden body 'wings' had already been popularized in Europe by the British company Status.

In 1986 the Gibson Guitar Corp agreed to buy Steinberger Sound and by 1990 had taken full control of the company. Ned acted as a consultant to Gibson for some time, working on stimulating products such as the Steinberger Transtrem transposing vibrato and the DB System detuner bridge. Recently, and with perhaps a hint of irony, Ned has

Vigier catalog c1986 (right)
Frenchman Patrice Vigier has produced
a number of unusual basses, such as
this model with 'delta metal'
fingerboard. Other oddities included the
Nautilus with an electronic method to
store and recall control settings, and
'10/90' necks made from 10 per cent
carbon graphite and 90 per cent wood.

Materials (below) Carbon reinforced
epoxy and phenolic resins were used for
body, neck and fingerboard.

**Jaydee Supernatural Classic
1978** (right) This belongs to Mark
King who used it on all the early Level
42 recordings and tours (King is seen in
action in the photo, above). John
Diggins ('JD') is the British maker who
built this Alembic-influenced instrument,
and it became the basis for Jaydee's
later Mark King model. King was widely
acclaimed for his thumb/slap style of
playing that fueled the pop-funk success
of Level 42 in the 1980s.

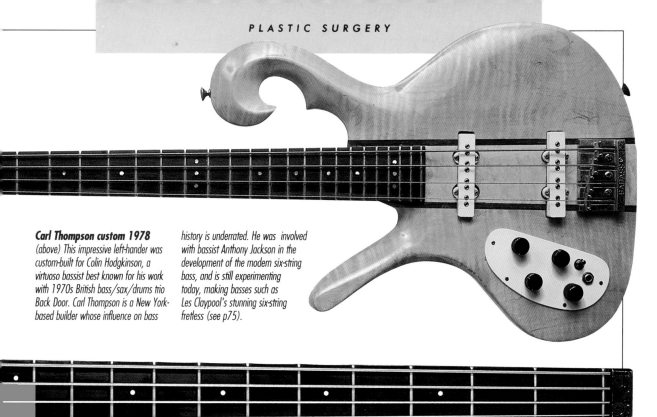

Carl Thompson custom 1978
(above) This impressive left-hander was custom-built for Colin Hodgkinson, a virtuoso bassist best known for his work with 1970s British bass/sax/drums trio Back Door. Carl Thompson is a New York-based builder whose influence on bass history is underrated. He was involved with bassist Anthony Jackson in the development of the modern six-string bass, and is still experimenting today, making basses such as Les Claypool's stunning six-string fretless (see p75).

Steinberger prototype 1979
(above and left) Ned Steinberger's first bass design had been the subtle Spector NS2 (p44/45), but this attempt was much more dramatic. He combined plastic materials, a radical new shape and active pickups in a design that quickly had musicians lining up to play the Steinberger L-2. The usual headstock was discarded, with tuners added to the body, which was trimmed down to the minimum. The bass pictured is the third of three prototypes, deemed good enough to debut at a 1979 instrument fair, and close but not identical to the production version: the back views of the prototype (top) and final version (below) show the small changes to shape and fittings.

Status Series II 1989 (left) UK maker Rob Green helped to popularize the headless concept and the carbon graphite through-neck style with added body 'wings', providing a more familiar styling that a number of bassists, particularly in Europe, found more appealing than Steinberger's mini-body.

been working on an electric upright bass design, the NS Double Bass.

STANLEY'S PICCOLO

Carl Thompson was a jazz guitarist who in 1967 began working in Dan Armstrong's guitar repair shop in New York. When Armstrong closed down some years later, Thompson says that many of the local players he'd worked for suggested he should open his own shop … which he did. Thompson continued to play jazz gigs, and on one occasion was asked to play bass, so he borrowed a Fender. Next day he complained to his partner Joel Frutkin about the shortcomings of the bass guitar, and Thompson began, as he puts it, "to think about making a real instrument". The thinking soon translated into action.

Consequently he and Frutkin began to build a small number of handmade bass guitars in 1974, and New York session players like Ken Smith became customers. "That same year I was very friendly with Stanley Clarke and Anthony Jackson," Thompson recalls. "Those guys were hanging out in the shop, they were playing club dates and record dates. I did some fret-jobs on Stanley's EB-2 and on his Alembics when he started playing those. Shortly after, when he first made the big-time, he came in and said he had this idea for making a bass that would be tuned up an octave, and did we think we could do it?"

Despite the fact that Thompson had made only around eight instruments at that point, he persevered with the idea and made the guitar that became known as a 'piccolo bass'. In some ways it wasn't a bass at all. It was tuned E-A-D-G but an octave higher than a bass: almost a guitar with two strings missing. However, the first piccolo bass that Thompson made for Clarke had the same 'full' 34in scale-length as a bass guitar. This, and the fact that it was devised by a bass player who played it with a bassist's technique, meant that it was more a high-tuned bass than anything else. Later, after the 34in piccolo bass was damaged, Thompson provided Clarke with a new 32in scale piccolo that became Clarke's main high-tuned bass. Clarke has continued to use an array of basses, including standard, tenor (up a fourth to A-D-G-C) and piccolo types,

and came to specialize in 'lead bass' playing, even going so far on some later performances as to employ an additional bassist to play conventional bass parts below Clarke's soloing.

Clarke first used piccolo bass on his best-selling *School Days* album, recorded in New York in June 1976, most obviously on the track 'Quiet Afternoon' where he played the main melody on the Carl Thompson 34in-scale piccolo bass (overdubbed above a conventional bass guitar part that he played on Alembic standard four-string). Carl Thompson remembers: "Stanley put my name on the back of that album and it kind of turned my life around. It made a lot of people aware that there was somebody on the scene called Carl Thompson."

EXTENDING THE BASS

Within a few weeks of Clarke coming in to his shop in 1974 with the piccolo request, Thompson was confronted with another seemingly peculiar idea when session player Anthony Jackson asked if it would be possible to make a six-string bass. However, Jackson was not thinking of the guitar-down-an-octave style of earlier six-strings, such as the Danelectro UB2 which had really been more of a guitar than a bass.

Jackson proposed to extend the bass guitar's range both upwards and downwards by keeping the standard four strings tuned E-A-D-G and adding a high C-string and a low B-string, resulting in a six-string bass tuned B-E-A-D-G-C. The high-C was not in itself a new idea for bass guitar: Fender had used it on their ill-judged and therefore short-lived Bass V (see page 34). But a low B-string was a new concept – and one that would later persuade many bassists to reach for the low notes. In 1974, however, it was a bizarre idea.

"There were many instances where I just wanted to go lower down," says Jackson about the origins of his low-B idea. "I would detune my Fender bass to get the lower notes when I wanted them, but it was always awkward to do that, it resulted in lower string tension which meant I had to raise the bridge, maybe modify the nut. There had to be an easier way to do that. I've always been a fan of pipe organ music, Bach, Messiaen, and I knew I could never hope to get any string as low as the lowest pipes on an organ. However, I felt that I ought to be able to get down another fourth, to B. I knew I was going to call it a contrabass guitar, because the range was below a bass guitar, enough to warrant a new name."

THE NEW SIX-STRING

It was difficult to find a maker willing to transform the idea into a guitar. Jackson had not yet climbed the heights of the session world that he would later reach (he worked with Steely Dan and Paul Simon among many others in the 1980s, for example) and so could not afford to experiment wildly with many expensive custom-made instruments. But Thompson agreed to go ahead and make a stab at the extended six-string bass – even though Jackson states that Thompson's initial reaction was that it was "a dumb idea".

Jackson says he left the details largely to Thompson, who recalls suggesting an extra-long scale-length but that Jackson opted for the 34in length he was used to from his Fender. Finding pickups wide enough to extend under all six strings proved almost impossible, but Atilla Zoller, a jazz guitarist with a flair for pickup building, was hired by Thompson to wind some custom units especially for the six-string. Thompson also had trouble finding a suitable bass string that would facilitate the low-B tuning, but the D'Addario string company eventually came up with a specially wound and suitably fat string.

The first extended-range six-string bass guitar finally appeared from Thompson's workshop early in 1975. Jackson was immediately disappointed by the string-spacing, which he had assumed was going to be wider. Later, into the 1980s, five- and six-string basses would become more popular and their string-spacing would become wider to suit the finger-style techniques of bassists rather than the plectrum-based styles of guitar players. However, in 1975 this was a brand new field, and no one was sure what to do. Jackson knew, however, that this first attempt at the contrabass guitar wasn't quite right.

He used it on a tour with Roberta Flack, laying down his Fender to play the new six on a couple of songs. "But I didn't

have a chance to put it through its paces until I did the first session with it," he says, "which was for the Panamanian saxophone player Carlos Garnett. We did an album called *Let This Melody Ring On* in June 1975, and on one particular tune I used the contrabass. I was absolutely adamant that Carlos should put in the credits 'Anthony Jackson bass guitar and contrabass guitar', which he did. I was very proud of that."

But Jackson abandoned the bass after that one tour and one recording session – primarily, he recalls, because he found the string-spacing restricting, and he returned to his Fender. Jackson and Thompson made some more experiments around 1976, including a fantastic 44in-scale trial bass guitar ("unimaginably large and completely unplayable!") and a 36in-scale four-string that Jackson did not keep for long. The musician and maker drifted apart, but Jackson continued to dream about the musical usefulness of an extended-range instrument. And he was not entirely alone.

TO B OR NOT TO B?

Jimmy Johnson was working as a freelance bass guitarist in Minneapolis, Minnesota, in the early-1970s doing jingles and other session work on his low-impedance, phase-switchable, short-scale Gibson Les Paul Bass. "I went to the music store and said it's a shame somebody can't make a long-scale bass with these kind of electronics in it," Johnson recalls. "And they said well, as a matter of fact, there's this company in California called Alembic. So I ordered a four-string Alembic, and this was how I found my way to custom instruments." Johnson was typical of many players who stumbled on Alembic in the early 1970s and discovered the new idea of the 'custom-made' bass – in other words, a one-off instrument built to the player's specifications. In the 1990s this is, of course, relatively commonplace, but back then it was a startlingly new concept.

Johnson, probably best known today for his work since 1990 with James Taylor, had been toying with the idea of an extended bass back in the mid-1970s that would enable him to play notes below the conventional low E-string, and he'd occasionally detuned his four-string as a means of venturing into lower-

57

58

Modulus catalog c1992 (above) Modulus Graphite was set up by Geoff Gould in the late 1970s.

Modulus Graphite Quantum six-string c1984 (above) Modulus was originally set up to develop the new idea of carbon graphite necks, which the company produced for Alembic, Music Man, Zon etc. The bass shown here has an extra-long 35in scale to help the fidelity of the low B-string, and features a tighter string spacing than most modern sixes. Note how the strings on this example mount directly into the body, underlining the profound strength of carbon graphite.

Jimmy Johnson (right) Session player Johnson ordered his five-string bass with low B-string from Alembic in 1975, one of the earliest 'modern' five-strings. The idea for a low-B five-string came from Johnson's father, an orchestral bass player who was familiar with low-note extensions fitted to some double-basses.

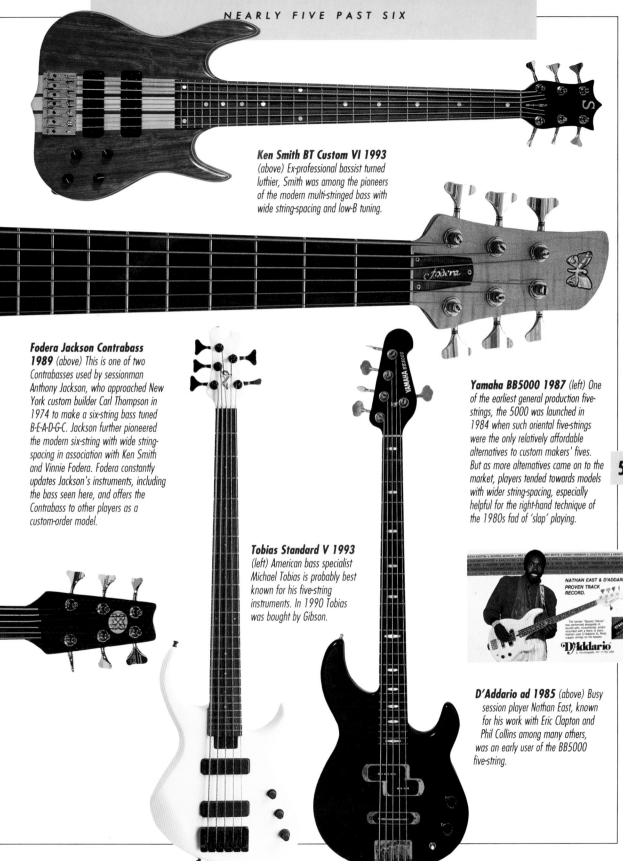

Ken Smith BT Custom VI 1993
(above) Ex-professional bassist turned
luthier, Smith was among the pioneers
of the modern multi-stringed bass with
wide string-spacing and low-B tuning.

**Fodera Jackson Contrabass
1989** (above) This is one of two
Contrabasses used by sessionman
Anthony Jackson, who approached New
York custom builder Carl Thompson in
1974 to make a six-string bass tuned
B-E-A-D-G-C. Jackson further pioneered
the modern six-string with wide string-
spacing in association with Ken Smith
and Vinnie Fodera. Fodera constantly
updates Jackson's instruments, including
the bass seen here, and offers the
Contrabass to other players as a
custom-order model.

Yamaha BB5000 1987 (left) One
of the earliest general production five-
strings, the 5000 was launched in
1984 when such oriental five-strings
were the only relatively affordable
alternatives to custom makers' fives.
But as more alternatives came on to the
market, players tended towards models
with wider string-spacing, especially
helpful for the right-hand technique of
the 1980s fad of 'slap' playing.

59

Tobias Standard V 1993
(left) American bass specialist
Michael Tobias is probably best
known for his five-string
instruments. In 1990 Tobias
was bought by Gibson.

D'Addario ad 1985 (above) Busy
session player Nathan East, known
for his work with Eric Clapton and
Phil Collins among many others,
was an early user of the BB5000
five-string.

pitched playing. His father, who played double-bass in the Minnesota orchestra, had an instrument fitted with a mechanical 'machine', a relatively common option for orchestral basses that consists of a headstock-mounted extension allowing the player to switch an extra-long 'E-string' down as low as C. At first Johnson and his father tried to figure a way of building a similar extension onto an electric bass guitar. They soon decided against this – but it's interesting to note that, once again, someone somewhere else was independently thinking along similar lines. The Kubicki company, founded by Philip Kubicki in California, launched their Ex-Factor electric bass guitar in the early 1980s with just such a headstock extension, giving the player the option of extending the lower reach of the E-string by two extra frets. Kubicki's stylish and ergonomically pleasing bass was described in the company's advertising as "the world's first electric extended bass", and was used by Stu Hamm to develop the independently coordinated two-hand tapping style of the late 1980s.

Back in the mid-1970s, Jimmy Johnson and his father were dissuaded from a similar 'extension' course, primarily by the comments of a string manufacturer. Johnson explains: "I contacted GHS at that time and asked them if it would be possible to get a very long low-E string for electric bass to suit our extension idea. I think they were part of my decision to go to a five-string rather than an extension, because they said it would be more difficult to make a long string than it would be to make a standard-length string with a wide diameter." Again from the influence of his father's orchestral background, Johnson was aware that some bass players used five-string double-basses with an extra low-B string.

In 1975 Johnson ordered a custom five-string from Alembic. He knew that they already offered such a model which they expected to supply with an additional high-C string, presumably for those who wanted to play occasional higher-pitched 'lead bass' parts. Johnson ordered a five-string on which he would modify the nut and bridge to take the special GHS low B-string, giving a B-E-A-D-G tuning. The Alembic

arrived in 1976, and was probably the first ever low-B five-string bass guitar. With increasingly wider string-spacing, the low-B five-string bass would become an important addition to the bass player's kit during the 1980s.

FOR THE CONNOISSEUR

Back on the east coast Anthony Jackson found a new bass-maker who agreed to build him another six-string 'contrabass' guitar. Ken Smith was a New Yorker who collected and dealt in double-basses and worked as a sessionman, playing double-bass and bass guitar on what he describes as "everything from Shirley Bassey and Broadway musicals to jingles and commercials". In the mid-1970s he'd begun to wonder why bass guitars couldn't be made to sound as pure and free of deadspots as the best double-basses. Smith had discussed these ideas with maker Carl Thompson, and as a result bought Thompson's third custom-made instrument. But still Smith thought he could do better, and resolved to start making bass guitars in his own right.

In late 1979 Smith had Thompson make up a rough 'carcass' bass from a design he'd sketched out. He took this bare-bones bass to Stuart Spector's workshop at the co-op loft in Brooklyn, and contracted Spector and co-worker Vinnie Fodera to produce the original Ken Smith basses. Fodera says that the first 32 Smith basses were made at Spector, "and the task fell largely to me". Spector remembers: "We were producing the finished woodwork and Smith was assembling them." Anthony Jackson bought one of these four-string basses, and meanwhile convinced Smith that he should produce for him a six-string contrabass guitar.

Smith decided to set up his own workshop in summer 1980, and logically asked Fodera to run the new shop. Fodera agreed, left Spector, had the Ken Smith workshop up and running by early 1981, and started work with a revised offset body shape for the new Ken Smith BT bass guitars (standing for 'Bass and Treble' after the active circuit fitted into them).

Fodera accurately specifies the importance of Ken Smith in the bass world of the early 1980s: "He might have been the first guy to give basses a kind of connoisseur attitude: he was a skilled musician designing and building his very own high quality original instruments, different from whatever else was on the market at the time, and bearing his own name. It was the first designer bass, if you will, at a very high price, and very exotic in every detail. He carried it further."

Jackson was now convinced that he needed wide string-spacing on the six-string. But Smith was not so sure, and the first Ken Smith six-string bass, built for Jackson at the end of 1981 by Fodera at the Smith shop, still had relatively narrow string-spacing. "It was much better than Carl's but the string spacing was too narrow," is Jackson's recollection of that bass. Nonetheless, he still managed to tour widely and record some 50 albums using it, and the bass became something of a research test-bed, with pickups and electric circuits being changed regularly. That bass was Jackson's sole tool from summer 1982, when he decided to leave the Fender at home and use the Smith six-string exclusively, on sessions such as those for Paul Simon's *Hearts And Bones* album.

THE CONTRABASS GUITAR

Jackson's second Ken Smith six-string came along in 1984, still with a 34in scale, but revised in terms of weight and feel, and with a small plate that noted it as a 'Smith-Fodera'. In order to have spacing between the strings similar to that of Jackson's Fender four-string *but across all six strings*, the bass was fitted with an extra-wide neck and fingerboard, and while this massive width looked decidedly odd, the bass was significant as the first extended-range six-string bass guitar with wide string-spacing. "I was very highly criticized by other instrument builders," says Ken Smith of the wide-spaced six, "by weight, by how wide this is – they said it looks like a battleship – but then a couple of years later they're all trying to chop into my business, only they're making 100 a week and I'm making two a week."

Its owner was very happy with this new contrabass guitar. "It was," concludes Jackson, "the first really viable instrument. I had realized the problem was in the wood and in the basic design of the first one, which was massive and heavy, and at the time everybody thought that was essential for sustain. I made a lot of recordings with this 1984 six-string, too, and it had the least deadspots of any instrument I'd ever played. It was a milestone," he says.

Fodera had parted from Smith in 1983, and acquired the existing workshop and continued to work from there, setting up Fodera Guitars with partner Joey Lauricella. But they carried on building Ken Smith basses under contract until 1985, and also began making their own Fodera bass guitars, including a low-B five-string model and, from 1986, six-string contrabass guitars for Jackson. At the time of writing Fodera Guitars had made Jackson a further three six-string basses, the last two of which are Jackson's current working instruments (the penultimate is shown on pages 58/59).

HOW LONG IS LONG?

The biggest change for these new Fodera six-strings was a move to an extra-long 36in scale, which improved the tone and tension of the low-B in particular. Around the mid 1980s Fodera was not alone in using an extra-long scale to facilitate low tuning: Modulus in the US used a 35in scale on their basses, while Overwater in England used a 36in scale for their C-Bass, a four-string tuned down two full tones to C-F-Bb-Eb. The 1985 C-Bass was designed in conjunction with Thompson Twins bassist Andrew Bodnar, who was looking for a stage instrument on which to reproduce low-pitched basslines that had been originated in the studio on synthesizers without consideration of the standard bass guitar's threshold of low-E.

Jackson blazed a trail for the six-string bass from those pioneering years of the first Carl Thompson experiments of the mid-1970s, but of greatest significance for the general development of the bass guitar was the additional low string, employed and popularized during the 1980s in the shape of the five-string bass guitar (tuned B-E-A-D-G). While the six-string bass has principally been put to use by players in the jazz and fusion fields, the five-string bass became an essential addition to the instruments carried by many touring and

61

Warwick Thumb 1993 (above) This is Jack Bruce's current Thumb bass. A successful German builder established in the 1980s by Hans-Peter Wilfer, son of Framus's founder, Warwick popularized waxed natural body finishes and bold styling features, some of which were clearly influenced by the Spector NS (see p44).

62

Kubicki ad 1983 (right) The stylish design of Kubicki's bass was reflected in the company's promotional material, this ad extolling the virtues of a bass that "comfortably interfaces with your body". The Ex-Factor is, it says, "the world's first electric extended bass", a reference to the fact that some acoustic double-basses had long been offered with a similar 'extension' feature.

PHILIP

THE HUMAN FACTOR
Designing an instrument to most comfortably interface with your body is a science called ergonomics. The EX FACTOR™ 4 combines these advanced principles with other unique features to present the world's first electric extended bass. For complete information, call or write to:

Philip Kubicki Guitar Technology
Box 40110
Santa Barbara, CA 93103
(805)963-6703

KUBICKI

Kubicki Ex-Factor 1990 (above) Californian maker Philip Kubicki launched the sleek Ex-Factor in 1983, its most unusual feature being the flick-lever on the headstock which gives a low two-fret extension to the E-string.

Roland G77 c1985 (above) This shortlived attempt at bass synthesis suffered from poor 'tracking', and did not translate clearly the low vibrations of bass strings into signals that a MIDI synthesizer needs to function accurately.

Ads mid-1980s (left) US maker Jackson (far left) popularized the use of colorful body graphics and the 'pointy' headstock. Note the emergence of the 'P/J' pickup layout: one split Precision-type plus Jazz bar unit. Fender (left) countered the growing number of oriental 'copies' by producing their own Japanese basses with the Squier brand.

Hamer 12-string Bass c1992 (above) This unusual instrument takes the multi-string bass just about as far as it can practically go. The 12 strings are arranged as four groups of three. Each trio consists of the normally tuned E, A, D or G string, plus two thinner strings tuned an octave above the norm.

The two octave strings are situated 'above' the normal string as the player looks down, although Hamer offer this bass with the octave strings 'below', and it provides a very full, ringing sound. This specialist item is still in production.

Hamer ad 1979 (left) Founded by Paul Hamer and Joel Dantzig in Illinois in the late 1970s, Hamer were closely associated with Cheap Trick (probably best known for their 'At Budokan' live album of 1979). Hamer made a variety of unusual custom instruments for bassist Tom Petersson as well as guitarist Rick Nielsen. Petersson is pictured left in this Hamer publicity shot with his 12-String Bass, modeled on an idea that the bassist had in 1977. Hamer also made some custom cutaway versions with soundholes.

recording bassists from all styles of music, and by the end of the decade a five-string model appeared on most self respecting bass-maker's pricelists. The low-B was here to stay.

SLAP THAT BASS

While other makers tested the suitability of graphite as a substitute material for the manufacture of bass necks, Travis Bean and Gary Kramer in California came up with a new alternative in the mid-1970s – aluminum. The Travis Bean basses and guitars had an aluminum neck that certainly proved resilient, and seemed to aid volume and sustain. But players did not like the cold feel of the metal against their hand, and the Travis Beans lasted only a few years in production. Bean's partner Kramer set up on his own over in New Jersey in 1975, and explored the use of other materials as an alternative to wood when he introduced basses with plastic 'ebonol' fingerboards. He also used aluminum necks, and while production of Kramer's instruments lasted longer than Bean's, cold aluminum still failed to win over too many players and the idea eventually faded.

Most innovative bassists of the 1970s preferred the familiar feel of wood in their hands, and among the players who stretched the musical horizons of bass guitar at that time were a pair of funk pioneers, Bootsy Collins and Bernard Edwards, who helped to define funk bass at either end of the decade. Bootsy did a colorful job in James Brown's band (he played the impossibly convoluted bassline on 'Sex Machine' 1970) as well as in George Clinton's wild P-Funk projects, using a strange star-shaped custom bass made by Larry Pletz. Edwards provided solid, undulating grooves within the smooth disco-funk of Chic (such as 'Good Times' 1979), primarily on Music Man and BC Rich basses.

Chris Squire played with British progressive rock band Yes, and his surging, bright, melodic lines did much for the rebirth of interest in Rickenbacker basses during the early 1970s. It was also in the 1970s that Larry Graham in Sly & The Family Stone (and in his own group Graham Central Station) used his Jazz Bass to popularize the 'slap' style of playing.

'Slapping' had been used for decades by some double-bass players, who would literally slap the strings with their picking hand in order to get more volume from their acoustic instruments. As the great Hollywood-musical lyricist Ira Gershwin put it in 1937: "Slap that bass, slap it till it's dizzy, slap that bass, keep the rhythm busy …" Many bass guitarists first noticed Larry Graham applying a modern version of the idea: using his right-hand he would bounce the edge of his thumb off one of the lower strings while also pulling higher strings, in various rhythmic combinations, generating a powerfully percussive sound. With its roots in 1970s funk, the bass guitar slap style also crossed over into jazz and fusion, but really took hold in the 1980s when it infiltrated all manner of musical styles and became required knowledge among bassists, even generating instructional books and videos dedicated entirely to its practice.

FENDER AFTER FENDER

The active electronics systems popularized in the early 1970s by Alembic began to find their way into less expensive instruments produced by other companies, and few with more success than Music Man. The company was established by Leo Fender and ex-Fender employees Forrest White and Tom Walker in 1972, originally as Tri-Sonics, then Musitek and finally, in 1974, as Music Man. When CBS had purchased the Fender companies they had given Leo a contract with a 10-year non-competition clause that expired in 1975, and in *The Music Trades* magazine dated April of that year Leo Fender was announced as president of Music Man Inc.

The first Music Man bass was the single-pickup StingRay with active electronics, the instrument being easily identified by its distinctive three-and-one tuner arrangement on the headstock (see page 51). Production of the StingRay started in June 1976: it was an almost instant hit, and remains popular to this day, considered by many players as a successful active update of Leo Fender's previous Precision Bass design. Music Man instruments were at first manufactured by Leo's CLF Research company in Fullerton, but after Music Man tried unsuccessfully to buy CLF in 1978 Leo decided to break away and set up his own new operation, G&L, in 1979.

Leo's associate Dale Hyatt remembers: "Leo told me he'd not had anything to do with Music Man since 1978, when he'd pulled out of it. He was still supposedly making guitars for them, but they had stopped all orders." By 1980 G&L had started production, and the company's output would include some fine basses such as the two-pickup active L2000 model. Music Man continued to make instruments in Fullerton for a while, but the company eventually folded and was sold to Ernie Ball in March 1984. Ernie Ball moved the operation north, near to Ball's existing string and accessory works in San Luis Obispo, where Music Man basses and guitars remain successfully in production today.

Early players of the Music Man StingRay in the 1970s underlined its versatility: Carl Radle used one in Eric Clapton's band throughout the decade to lay down effortless rock grooves, while Louis Johnson of The Brothers Johnson proved the Music Man's worth in funk, popularizing its suitability for the slap style of bass playing (primarily through the use of the on-board battery-powered active electronics that enabled the bass and treble tones to be boosted, resulting in a sound with much reduced middle frequencies when compared to the passive Precision Bass). And in 1983 Pino Palladino's lyrical fretless StingRay pricked up listeners' ears when it was featured prominently on the introduction to Paul Young's hit version of Marvin Gaye's 'Wherever I Lay My Hat (That's My Home)'.

LOOK ... NO FRETS

The name of Jaco Pastorius has become almost synonymous with the fretless bass guitar, for it was in his hands during the late 1970s that the instrument came alive for the first time. Not that Pastorius was by any means the first player to use fretless bass, but he popularized its sound by bringing it right up front, playing it in a virtuosic manner as a featured instrument.

The fretless bass, with its smooth, unfretted fingerboard, enables bassists to achieve a sound that is completely different from that of the fretted instrument: notes 'swell' with a beautifully warm tone and the fretless player can easily execute an impressive slide (sometimes called a 'gliss', short for glissando) or incorporate longitudinal string vibrato into his sound. To obtain similar sounds, some players had tried electric upright basses of the early-1960s, such as the double-bass-shaped Ampeg Baby Bass or the more skeletal German-built Framus Triumph Bass, nicknamed the 'pogo stick', but neither proved very successful.

Among the earliest well-known players of fretless bass guitar was Rick Danko of American folk-rock pioneers The Band. Danko was primarily a fretted Fender player, but was given a number of instruments by Ampeg around 1970 including an AUB-1 fretless bass guitar which he quickly modified with Fender pickups. "I used the Ampeg on about 80 per cent of our *Cahoots* album of 1971," recalls Danko, who also used it for the end-of-1971 concert that became the *Rock Of Ages* live album. "It's a challenge to play fretless," he specifies, "because you have to really use your ear."

Another early exponent of the fretless bass was Ralphe Armstrong, who used a hybrid Fender with Jazz body and fretless Precision neck during his tenure with John McLaughlin's Mahavishnu Orchestra (on *Apocalypse* 1974 and *Visions Of The Emerald Beyond* 1975), and later with Jean-Luc Ponty. While it was primarily in jazz-rock that the instrument first took hold, the distinctive sound did spread to other styles, and a striking, influential appearance of the instrument in pop music occurred on Bad Company's summer 1974 hit single 'Can't Get Enough', with Boz Burrell's fretless Precision well to the fore.

John Francis Pastorius III was born in Norristown on the outskirts of Philadelphia, Pennsylvania, in 1951 and moved with his family to Fort Lauderdale, Florida, eight years later. His father was a professional drummer and 'Jaco' took up the instrument too, joining a teenage jazz band at the age of 13 and moving to bass guitar in 1967. He moved on to a variety of pro work, everything from touring with R&B bands to playing cruise-ship MOR, but in 1975 his dues paid off and Jaco took a giant step, recording with Pat Metheny on the jazz

Overwater C Bass 1988 (left) While other makers offer five-string basses to provide extra low notes, UK maker Chris May built this model with an extra-long 36in scale facilitating tuning two tones below standard (C-F-Bb-Eb).

TUNE GUITAR TECHNOLOGY

Tune ad c1992 (above) The Tune company was founded in Japan in the early 1980s by bass maker and designer Fugitani Hatzukazu.

Guild Ashbory 1987 (above) This tiny 22in-scale bass has rubber strings and a bridge piezo pickup. Designed by Alun Jones and Nigel Thornbory in the UK, it was originally made by Guild. Remarkably enough it produces a very convincing double-bass sound.

Tune Bass Maniac c1991 (left) Tune's founder Fugitani Hatzukazu had previously been involved with the production of Fender replicas for another Japanese company, but set up his own operation in order to produce other designs. The 25-fret Bass Maniac, introduced in 1983, was notable for the access it gave players to the upper frets, made possible by an extended neck with 'heel-less' joint. The overall style and ergonomics of the Tunes were widely copied in the 1980s, primarily by other oriental makers.

Pedulla Pentabuzz 1994 (left) A five-string fretless is not the most common combination, but US maker Michael Pedulla is well known for his fretless basses, typically with sculpted body horns and distinctive lacquered fingerboards. The ad (below right) relates to the percussive 'slapping' style of playing, while bassist Mark Egan (below left) plays a Pedulla twin-neck.

Love at first slap.

Find out why the MVP bass is such a hit. Send $3 for a color catalog.

Pedulla
The Serious Bass
M.V. Pedulla Guitars, Box 226, Rockland, MA 02370, USA. (617) 871-0073.

Zemaitis 1988 (right) Tony Zemaitis has been making custom electric guitars and basses in the UK since 1975, and is best known for distinctive instruments with engraved metal pickguards, as on this example. Users like 'Plonk' Lane of The Faces and various Rolling Stones have periodically given Zemaitis a high profile.

guitarist's *Bright Size Life* album, nobably on 'Round Trip/ Broadway Blues'.

In 1976 Jaco joined the jazz-rock group Weather Report, with whom he stayed for six eventful years. The band had been formed in 1971 by keyboardist Joe Zawinul and sax player Wayne Shorter, both of whom had been members of the experimental jazz-rock lineups of the Miles Davis band in the late 1960s. There they had acquired a taste for the fusion of rock's amplified rhythms and the moody freedom of modal jazz, a combination they developed in Weather Report.

Jaco's pioneering use of the fretless bass guitar with its singing, sustained quality and his tremendous harmonic and melodic skills on the instrument coincided with some of Weather Report's finest recorded compositions and daringly improvisational live work, nearly always with Pastorius's bass prominently positioned in the mix. The band became one of the most commercially successful jazz-rock outfits, and probably their best known piece from the period is 'Birdland' from *Heavy Weather* (1977), an intricate weave of sounds and textures enlivened by Jaco's strong bass work.

However, most bass players had their earliest encounter with the sounds of Jaco's playing when they heard his first solo album, *Jaco Pastorius*, released in 1976. On this he used the two Fender Jazz Basses that stayed with him for most of his career, a fretted 1960 model and a de-fretted 1962. He played the fretless '62 on most of the tracks on the solo album, including the captivating double-tracked 'Continuum' that defined the Jaco fretless sound, while the fretted Jazz appeared on just two tracks, 'Come On, Come Over' and the much-imitated 'Portrait Of Tracy' that demonstrated Jaco's remarkable use of harmonics. ('Natural harmonics', to give them their full correct name, are ringing high-pitched notes produced by touching rather than fretting strategic points on the strings.)

JACO: JAZZ: GENIUS

Pastorius said in a 1976 interview that he'd been using both his Jazz basses since about 1971. As he paid only $90 for the secondhand 'fretless' Jazz it seems unlikely that he could have

afforded a new bass – but in fact there wouldn't have been many new fretless basses for him to have chosen from in 1971. About all that was available in the US were two fretless models that had been launched the previous year: Hohner's XK250 semi-solid fretless bass (listed at $395 new) and the Fender Precision Fretless (various versions from $293 to $321). The Hohner made little impression, while the Fender was generally poorly received: on one hand double-bass players felt that its sound was too muffled and ill-defined; on the other hand bass guitarists found the Fretless hard to play in tune.

So it was that some players keen to achieve a fretless sound had no choice but to unlock their toolkits and take matters into their own hands. Pastorius said in 1976 that someone had already removed the frets from the '62 Jazz when he bought it. "Looked like somebody had taken a hatchet to it, so I had to fix it up," he laughed. Jaco painted glossy epoxy over the defretted fingerboard to give it a smooth feel. "I've always been playing fretless bass, and I've had a few other fretless basses that I had to take the frets out of myself," he said.

Pastorius complained in that interview that the sliding, growling bass sounds on his 1976 solo album had meant that some listeners – few of whom had probably heard a fretless bass or even knew that such a thing existed – had assumed that he must have been playing double-bass. Jaco had tried double-bass without success, he explained: "It's a pain in the ass, it's just too much work for too little sound. I love to play with drummers, and it's next to impossible to play upright bass with a drummer. No matter how loud you get you're not loud enough," he added.

Despite Jaco's post-Weather Report band Word Of Mouth as well as his notable contributions to Joni Mitchell's *Hejira* (1976) and her live *Shadows And Light* (1980), his career was to be tragically short-lived, and following drug-related problems he died in September 1987 aged just 35. Strangely, Fender had done nothing to capitalize on the success and popularity of Pastorius, and rather surprisingly did not produce a fretless Jazz Bass at the time; such apparently obvious marketing was left largely to oriental makers and custom builders who were happy to supply such basses. But it was Jaco who opened many players' ears to a whole new world of possibilities from the fretless bass guitar, and any number of bassists could be heard in the 1980s 'doing a Jaco' by playing prominent, melodic fretless basslines – whether on production fretless instruments or do-it-yourself de-fretted basses. Some brave bassists found that they preferred a fretless with a plain, unmarked fingerboard, while others opted for the reassurance of inlaid lines where the frets would normally have been (the 'lined fretless', as it became known).

ORIENTAL INFLUENCE

At the beginning of the 1980s Japanese-made bass guitars were growing in importance and becoming more accepted. When the Japanese had started emulating classic American guitars in the early 1970s, most western makers didn't see much to worry about. Later, the quality of these oriental instruments improved, but some American makers still kept their heads stuck firmly in the sand. As Dave Gupton, vice president of Fender in 1978, commented at the time: "Fender is not adversely affected by the Japanese copies as perhaps some of the other major manufacturers, because we have been able to keep our costs pretty much in line."

That casual attitude changed dramatically in a few short years. By the dawn of the 1980s the dollar had soared in value relative to the yen. Coupled with the high quality of many Japanese basses, this meant that instruments built in the orient were making a real impact on the market. Several Japanese companies made real leaps in design and construction, and had taken on board some of the ideas of high-end US producers – including specific features such as the active electronics and visible through-neck of Alembic, or more general trends such as low-B five-string basses – and incorporated them into more affordable instruments. They included Ibanez (with their Musician series as used by Sting), Aria (used by several British bassists including John Taylor of Duran Duran and Neil Murray of Whitesnake) and Yamaha (whose BB5000 narrow-spaced five-string was a strong seller

in the US thanks to the influence of players like Nathan East).

THE EIGHTIES BASS BOOM

By the first few years of the 1980s the bass guitar – whether it was made in the US, Japan, Europe or elsewhere – had come of age. Since its birth some 30 years earlier, the electric bass had been provided with many new facilities that established the instrument more than ever before as an essential part of the process of contemporary music making. As bassist Jeff Berlin wrote in his regular 'Bass And Beyond' column in *Guitar Player* magazine in March 1984: "Look what's happening to the electric bass these days. The instrument is becoming more modernized all the time. They're building four-string, five-string, six-string, eight-string, fretless, piccolo and two-octave basses; basses with thick necks, thin necks and graphite necks, plastic bodies, wood bodies, *no* bodies; and every conceivable combination of strings, bridges, pickups, tone and volume controls (both active and passive), tuning pegs, strap locks, and even nut pieces."

Clearly a revolution had taken place among musicians and manufacturers, and the industry must have been delighted to see a boom in sales during the 1980s as the bass guitar became the hip instrument of the moment and a glut of successful bassists highlighted its new-found versatility and prominence. In Europe it was Mark King who personified this fresh cult of the bass. As the talented bass-playing frontman for Level 42, who had a stream of Top-10 hits from 1984 onwards, King at first played his funky slap style on a British Alembic-influenced Jaydee bass (pictured on pages 54/55). King led a whole new generation of players to take up the evidently enjoyable, popular and hugely fashionable bass guitar.

In the US Billy Sheehan came to prominence in the pop-metal band of singer David Lee Roth, where he cheerfully battled it out with Roth's guitarist Steve Vai, and Sheehan established himself from the mid 1980s onward as a bass hero, much in the mold of the guitar hero of years past. His eccentrically modified Fender bass was marketed as the Attitude model by Yamaha, and Sheehan consistently topped

69

Steinberger Q4 c1990 (right) This more conventional looking and wooden-bodied Steinberger provides further evidence that many bassists want conformity in their instruments. Steinberger's headless design will survive, but the mini-body of his original bass has proved less durable.

Steinberger XM2 c1989 (left) The XM was co-designed by guitar-maker Roger Giffin and (tall) Genesis bassist Mike Rutherford, who felt that Steinberger's mini-body (see p54/55) looked too tiny on him. The XM2 shown has the optional Transtrem fitted, a special unit with a slotted ratchet protruding from the pivoted bridge. Moving the arm positions the bridge at preset angles, changing the length and therefore the pitch of all the strings.

Ovation Elite 5 1994 (right) Ovation have been making their famous bowl-back electro-acoustic guitars since 1966, but only recently have they introduced a bass version, first in four-string format and later adding a five-string. Reproducing an acoustic low B-string is certainly a challenge, but owner Dave Bronze proved the value of this bass when he used it on a number of tracks on Eric Clapton's 'From The Cradle' blues album of 1994. The multiple soundholes on the body and the distinctive rounded fiberglass back (see side view, far right) aid the Ovation's acoustic projection; body-mounted controls govern the electric sound of the bridge-mounted transducer.

70

Q4 bridge (right) The flick-lever seen here on the low E-string is Steinberger's contribution to the recent trend toward detuning. Some players find it musically useful to lower the E-string to D, and gadgets like this one mechanize what had always been a manual operation. Kubicki's unit (see p62) does a similar job at the headstock, where some players choose to retrofit Hipshot's 'D-tuner'.

Washburn ad 1991 (above) The Washburn brandname dates back to Chicago in the 1870s, but recent products are of US design and oriental manufacture. These include the AB electro-acoustic bass models, publicized here by players like Darryl Jones (center) who replaced Bill Wyman in the Rolling Stones for the group's 1994 world tour.

Martin B-65 1990 (left) Despite their traditional image as the oldest American maker of acoustic guitars, the Martin company had dabbled unsuccessfully with solidbody basses in the late 1970s. More recently they joined the electro-acoustic bass trend with typically understated flair.

Guild ad 1990 (above) Guild started in the guitar business in the 1950s, and the company's reputation was built primarily on flat-top acoustic guitars. In 1975 they started making one of the earliest acoustic basses (see also Earthwood, p45) and have more recently offered the inevitable electro versions, as seen in this brochure.

71

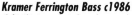

Kramer Ferrington Bass c1986 (left) This is a relatively early example of an electro-acoustic bass, designed for Kramer by US custom maker Danny Ferrington. Unlike the traditional Martin style (above), this model obviously comes from an electric guitar maker: note the 1980s 'pointy' headstock and the body outline clearly based on an electric. Built into the bridge is a piezo-electric pickup (often called a 'transducer', which actually describes any kind of pickup). The piezo pickup incorporates special crystals that generate a signal when they detect movement in the guitar's top as well as in the strings. In this way it is intended to reproduce more of the acoustic character of the sound than would a normal magnetic pickup.

popularity polls throughout the world by virtue of his accomplished playing skills and diligent self-promotion.

Pop fans and bass players alike were drawn to King and Sheehan, but in the pure Musicians' Musician stakes of the 1980s few bassists performed better than Marcus Miller and John Patitucci. While both men made fine solo records, Miller applied the popular slap style to jazz most publicly on several 1980s recordings and tours of the tirelessly experimental trumpeter and bandleader Miles Davis, using a modified Jazz Bass (see page 29) and, later, instruments by Sadowsky and Modulus. Meanwhile Patitucci's work on double-bass and on six-string bass guitar (primarily on a Ken Smith and later a Yamaha TRB model) was highlighted through his dates and sessions with jazz keyboard player Chick Corea's band, such as the *Inside Out* album (1990).

PULLING THE PLUG

MTV, the music satellite-TV channel, started to broadcast a series in the late 1980s called *Unplugged*, capitalizing on the rise in popularity of acoustic music at the time. The first *Unplugged* was broadcast in November 1989, featuring Squeeze with Syd Straw and Elliot Easton, and as more programs followed, 'unplugged' quickly became a catchphrase that summed up a musical trend.

The idea of the TV program was that rock bands better known for loud, amplified work would unplug their electric equipment and play a concert with acoustic instruments. This proved surprisingly successful: many musicians clearly reveled in the opportunity to unplug and go acoustic, even if only for the one gig, and fans welcomed the appearance of a new slant on well-known material. As far as the musical instrument industry was concerned, the popularity of acoustic music in general and *Unplugged* in particular gave a new lease on life to the sales of acoustic instruments.

Acoustic was in vogue, and air began to appear inside all manner of guitars – including basses. Consider for a moment an electric guitarist picking up a flat-top acoustic guitar. At that point he connects with a tradition that goes back at the

very least to the Martin company's innovations early in the 20th century. But when the acoustic bass guitar had first begun to appear in the 1970s it was a new hybrid instrument with no historical background, combining bass guitar stringing and tuning with a flat-top acoustic guitar's construction. Ironically, this initial combination only served to re-introduce one of the very problems the electric bass guitar had been designed to eliminate: that the inherent lack of volume of a pure acoustic instrument can only be increased by enlarging the size of the body, often to unmanageable proportions.

The huge dimensions of an established Mexican acoustic bass instrument, the guitarrón, inspired one of the earliest acoustic bass guitars, the vast Earthwood Bass of 1972 (pictured on page 45), built by the Ernie Ball company on the US west coast. Other acoustic bass guitars followed in the 1970s, including models made by Guild in the US and Eko in Italy. In order to increase the volume of these hybrid acoustic basses, both companies offered optional versions with bridge-mounted pickups to provide a novel amplified-acoustic sound.

It was primarily this type of 'electro-acoustic' bass that became popular as the *Unplugged* acoustic boom began to reverberate around the late 1980s – when in fact 'acoustic' often meant acoustic only in looks and feel, because in reality amplification still had to be used to project most performances. The new breed of electro-acoustic basses had thin bodies and bridge pickups, and the first to appear had been the Kramer Ferrington in 1986.

Guitar-maker Danny Ferrington was a custom-builder who in the mid-1980s struck a licensing deal with the Kramer guitar company of New Jersey, who were looking for some acoustic designs to sell to their decidedly electric clientele. First up was an electro-acoustic guitar in 1985, followed by a bass the following year. "They had standard electric-style necks on a thin acoustic body," Ferrington remembers of the Kramer Ferrington pointed-headstock models. "It was Kramer's way of getting to electric players, because acoustic was getting big then but some players still thought you had to be a folkie or something. So I thought: make it small and slim, with the same access and feel as an electric bass." And that's exactly what he did. The Kramer Ferrington debuted at a US musical instrument show early in 1986. Ferrington: "We were the first with a thin acoustic bass with a pickup that you could play like a bass guitar. By the June show Washburn had one, and by the following year everyone seemed to have them. I thought ours was a real nice design. Fleetwood Mac and Aerosmith used it on video, and The Cure used it on their *Unplugged* show, because it looked a bit different from the ordinary."

PIEZO PRESSURE

Most makers of modern electro-acoustic basses use piezo-electric pickups mounted into the instrument's bridge, a system that had been established by Ovation in the late-1960s. This type of pickup incorporates special crystals that generate electricity under mechanical strain and as a result pick up the vibration of the guitar's top as well as the individual strings. The sound produced by a piezo-electric pickup is therefore different from that generated by the normal electric bass guitar's magnetic pickup, which responds solely to metal strings moving in its magnetic field. In theory at least, the piezo should give more 'acoustic' character in its amplified sound. One of the attractions of an electro-acoustic bass is that it provides bass guitarists with the opportunity of obtaining something approaching a double-bass sound. A closer approximation was achieved by the Ashbory bass (at one time produced by Guild) which featured rubber strings stretched over a tiny 22in scale, and a piezo pickup. In the hands of players such as Doug Wimbish and Tony Levin the odd-looking Ashbory produced a remarkably convincing double-bass emulation, all the more strange given its small size.

Electro-acoustic basses from makers like Kramer and Washburn among others could be seen fueling the *Unplugged* shows and spin-offs, and many artists were blessed with extra record and video sales when recordings of the concerts were released. One of the biggest beneficiaries was Eric Clapton, whose *Unplugged* album of 1992 did much to underline his popularity and landed him no less than six of the music

industry's coveted Grammy awards. Clapton's bassist Nathan East, who adopted a Guild acoustic bass as well as an upright bass for their *Unplugged* show, recalls: "We did a lot of new material that hadn't been recorded, and a completely different version of 'Layla', a jazzier, bluesier version. Things just take on a completely different shape when they're in that acoustic state, and it was a refreshing change of pace."

ELECTRONIC BASS

In sharp contrast to the acoustic trend, some manufacturers began to link together the bass guitar and the synthesizer during the 1980s to make a new electronic instrument, the bass guitar synthesizer (usually referred to as a 'bass synth').

It was not an entirely new idea to try to make a bass sound like a keyboard: British maker Vox had developed a daring if unreliable Guitar Organ in the mid-1960s and made at least one prototype bass version. But as keyboard synthesizers evolved in the 1970s some makers of these instruments saw the possibility of applying the technology to existing instruments. In some quarters there was a feeling – not entirely unjustified as it turned out – that synthesizers would oust 'traditional' electric guitars and basses as the primary instruments of pop music-making.

Ampeg, never too far from bass innovation, teamed up with the Swedish guitar maker Hagstrom in the late 1970s to produce an early guitar synthesizer system, the Patch 2000, and while a bass version is shown in their catalog it does not seem to have reached production. But it was Roland, a leading Japanese synthesizer manufacturer established in 1974, who brought the bass synth to market.

Roland began experiments with guitar synthesizers in the late 1970s. They developed the concept of a special guitar (they called it a 'controller') plus a separate box containing most of the synthesizer circuitry. Two bass systems appeared: the relatively conventional-looking G33 or G88 (1980) and the futuristic G77 (1985; pictured on page 63) which had a strongly angular body and a plastic neck-strengthening spar running parallel to the neck. The bass guitars were made for

Body (below) Exactly 40 years after his innovative Precision, Leo Fender still found that original shape inspiring.

G&L six-string bass prototype 1991 (above) This is the bass on which Leo Fender was working on the day he died. In contrast to modern six-string basses, the instrument is essentially a guitar pitched an octave lower than normal, something of a reversion to the style of Fender's Bass VI (see p23). Perhaps Leo was looking back for inspiration to his classic Fenders of the 1950s and 1960s?

Leo Fender's G&L workshop (above) The workshop at G&L's headquarters on East Fender Avenue in Fullerton, Los Angeles, has been left exactly as it was on the day that Leo Fender died in March 1991. Leo worked in this room on the six-string bass prototype shown above.

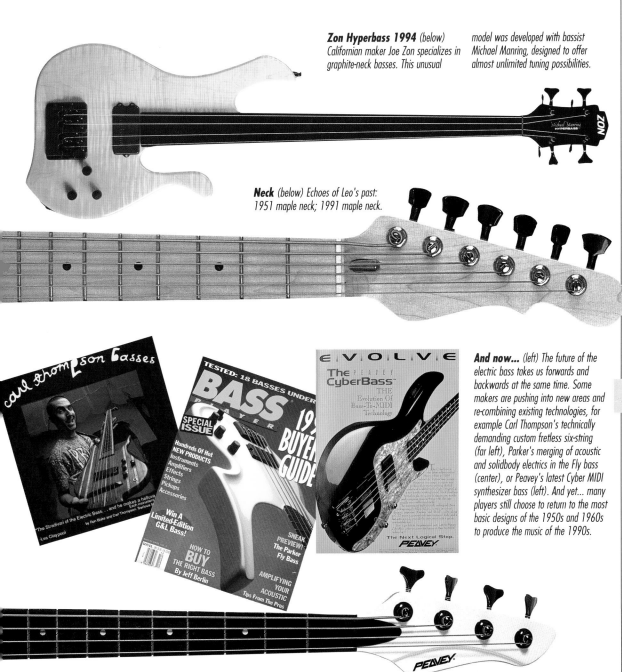

Zon Hyperbass 1994 (below) Californian maker Joe Zon specializes in graphite-neck basses. This unusual model was developed with bassist Michael Manring, designed to offer almost unlimited tuning possibilities.

Neck (below) Echoes of Leo's past: 1951 maple neck; 1991 maple neck.

And now... (left) The future of the electric bass takes us forwards and backwards at the same time. Some makers are pushing into new areas and re-combining existing technologies, for example Carl Thompson's technically demanding custom fretless six-string (far left), Parker's merging of acoustic and solidbody electrics in the Fly bass (center), or Peavey's latest Cyber MIDI synthesizer bass (left). And yet... many players still choose to return to the most basic designs of the 1950s and 1960s to produce the music of the 1990s.

Peavey Midibase 1993 (above) Makers have long attempted to provide a bass guitar that will interface accurately and reliably with a synthesizer to open the door to the range of tones and sounds that the electronic instrument offers. This bass from US maker Peavey attempts the job by triggering the synthesizer from sensors built into the fingerboard.

Roland by Fuji Gen-Gakki, also known for producing some Ibanez and Fender/Squier basses.

MIDI BASS

Roland maintained faith in the idea: for many years the company developed their bass synth and tried to create a market while no other manufacturers seemed confident or even interested enough to provide any real competition. Significantly, bass players were in general unconvinced by the Roland, largely due to its inherent inability to immediately identify and reproduce all notes accurately. The Roland bass synth used a pitch-to-voltage technique that tries to analyze the waveform of a vibrating string. From that it should in theory immediately determine the frequency and send a corresponding signal to the synthesizer. In reality the system usually takes a few discernible milliseconds as it attempts to 'read' the low frequency bass notes, because it takes time to register a relatively slowly vibrating bass string. This crucial hesitation is known as MIDI delay. (MIDI is the Musical Instrument Digital Interface used by most synthesizer manufacturers since the 1980s.)

One bassist who bravely used a Roland bass synth to 'play' sampled digital sounds was Dave Bronze, who used a G77 with British sampling pioneers The Art Of Noise on a 1986 tour. "Because of the infamous MIDI delay," he recalls, "which gets worse the lower down you go, I transposed all the bass samples down an octave and played everything up an octave, which reduced the delay. We just about got away with it. The odd thing was that after doing that eight-week world tour, when I went back to normal bass I found I was playing ahead of the beat all the time. I had to work with a metronome and learn to play on or behind the beat again."

Most players were not willing to make these compromises in order to achieve sounds that could be made much more easily and reliably with keyboard instruments, and the Roland units faded from the scene. Meanwhile Steve Chick, an Australian bassist and electrical engineering graduate, was getting bored in his air-conditioning job and started amusing himself in the

evenings by putting together a bass synthesizer. This would in time become the MIDI Bass system, incorporated into basses by makers such as Wal in England and Valley Arts in the US, and which later became the foundation of the Peavey Midibase and CyberBass models. But in 1982 it was just a hobby for Chick. "I was a bass player and I knew what I wanted," he recalls. "But it was only for me – I had a hankering to get back into music and I thought an instrument like this could give me a real edge. There was never really any commercial idea to it whatsoever."

Chick had seen the Roland system and noted its shortcomings. "So I immediately discounted those pitch-to-voltage techniques," he remembers, "and realized that there had to be some other way to tell what the pitch of the string was." Working on his own with no commercial considerations, Chick figured that an electronic sensing system built into the frets of the bass was the way forward.

"It seemed to make more sense to work off string position than measuring the vibrations," says Chick. "So I ended up developing a neck with split frets to work out where your fingers were, and from that the system could tell what string and what note you were playing. I also used a pickup to measure the dynamics of the string so I could see when the note was struck and when the note decayed. The fret-sensing and the pickup information were combined into a small computer that put the two together and generated MIDI to drive a synthesizer," he explains.

BASSISTS VS SCIENTISTS

The Australian guitar company Maton briefly released a commercial system in 1985, but Chick soon started his Bass Technology company, putting out their own MIDI Bass unit in 1986, the MB4 – it was this 'retrofit' system that was supplied to Wal, Valley Arts and others. Bass Technology folded in 1989, at which point Chick decided to redesign his bass synth system from scratch. "I spent 1990 engineering it from the ground up again," he says, "trying to utilize all the new things I'd learned during the years, making it programmable, and trying to address all the negatives that people had: some wanted pitchbend, for example. I was aiming to get a license deal with a big company, and it eventually went to Peavey in the US in 1991," says Chick

Peavey's Midibase was launched in 1992, the system coming as a reasonably conventional looking bass guitar with accompanying rackmount interface that would drive a separate synthesizer of the player's choice. *Bass Player* magazine ran a review of the new instrument soon after it appeared. "Hearing a flute or organ coming from your bass takes some getting used to, but it's pretty addictive," wrote Karl Coryat, noting that the instrument flawlessly translated most of his playing into accurate synth notes, aside from a few carelessly articulated runs. "The Midibase can be very complex when it comes to programming and configuring the system," concluded Coryat, "[but] if you like high tech and are eager to explore the possibilities of new sounds, this bass is for you."

Early in 1994 Peavey changed the instrument's name to CyberBass after a company proved prior use of 'Midibase'. Still to establish itself widely, the Peavey bass synth is a brave step that at least allows bass players the facility to use their chosen instrument as a way into contemporary digital composing and sound-generating systems, should they feel that such a course is worthwhile. "I think the success of this project has been through working with bass players continually," says Chick, "rather than having scientists in white coats saying oh, bassists will like this. It's not a simple instrument, and it's going to take time. The thing that keeps me going is thinking about Leo Fender. He was building Fender basses for years before things really started getting moving."

HIGH-TECH OR LOW GROOVE?

Picture the bass guitarist of the 1990s, faced with a multitude of choices. It might be that he could use all this modern technology, or take advantage of makers still attempting the next ground-breaking step, perhaps with altered tunings or the combination of acoustic and solidbody electrics. Maybe he could discipline himself to master a different technique on extended-range, fretted or fretless bass? Nonetheless, the

significant trend for the bass guitarist of the 1990s has been to return to the roots, to grab an old Fender and lay down the groove – confirming, remarkably, that Leo Fender pretty much got the design right first time out.

This cyclical turn of events is easier to understand now that we have studied the astounding progress of the bass guitar in its relatively short lifespan. For almost ten years from the bass guitar's launch in 1951 manufacturers were unconvinced of its commercial potential, and many had trouble deciding whether or not to produce one. Even when they did, recording engineers and band leaders hesitated to use it, and musicians weren't sure if it was an instrument for double-bass players or for guitarists.

But with the dramatic explosion of pop music in the early 1960s, the task of who *would* play this unfashionable background instrument rapidly developed into who *could* play the alternative styles and demanding techniques of later years.

The development of the instrument has been led by players. From bass guitarists came the inspiration for fretless bass, the idea for five- and six-string bass guitars, the demand for lighter strings to play slap style, even the pioneering spirit behind the MIDI Bass. These ideas were encouraged by the Alembic-influenced concept of the custom builder working to individual musicians' requirements, and were often taken further by the larger instrument companies with their full production and promotional facilities.

Consequently the bassist has become used to change and open to suggestions. So when new design ideas came along, such as the alternative materials and headless instruments of Steinberger in the 1980s, they were not dismissed but welcomed as useful new developments of the modern bass.

The bass guitar now exists in many forms. One extreme is the sophisticated high-tech bass that might combine graphite technology, state-of-the-art electronics and exotic woods, while at the other end of the scale is the instrument in its original, simple, understated form. Both stand side by side with equal importance to the bass guitarist of the 1990s, and will undoubtedly continue to do so.

March 24, 1953   C. L. FENDER   Des. 169,062
                            GUITAR
                      Filed Nov. 21, 1952

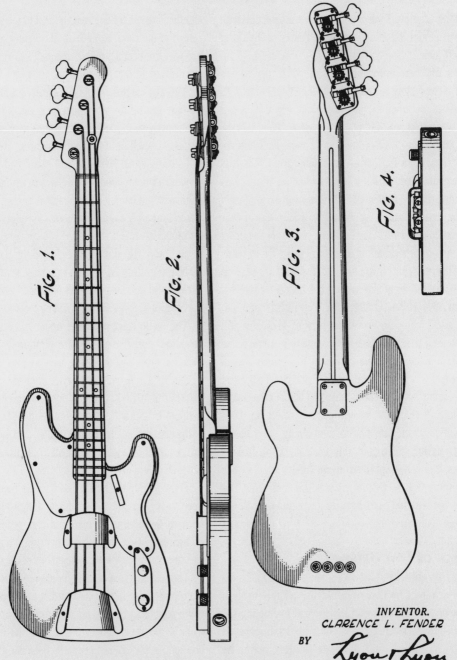

Fig. 1.   *Fig. 2.*   *Fig. 3.*   *Fig. 4.*

INVENTOR.
CLARENCE L. FENDER
BY
Lyon & Lyon
ATTORNEYS

REFERENCE SECTION

REFERENCE LISTING

This closing section (pages 82-103) uses a simple, condensed format to convey a large amount of information about the bass guitars produced by 46 companies. The notes here are intended to ensure that you gain the most from this unique inventory.

Manufacturers are included in the Reference Listing if they have a bass pictured in *The Bass Book* (not including shots in publicity material etc). The 'Big Six' bass makers – Alembic (p82), Fender (p85), Gibson (p90), Music Man (p96), Rickenbacker (p98) and Steinberger (p101) – have been given comprehensive coverage, listing main model entries for their principal bass guitars and a summary of the rest of their output. The other 40 companies, from Ampeg to Zon, are provided with a main model entry/entries for the instrument(s) pictured in *The Bass Book*, plus a brief round-up of other basses they have produced. Custom makers who produce few or no specific models are necessarily given a less detailed listing. If you can't find a company or brand immediately, try looking them up in the index (pages 104-107).

In the main model entries, the company's brandname appears in a block at the head of the listing. For the 'Big Six' this is followed by a list of features that are assumed to be common to all bass guitars made by that company, to avoid too much repetition in the entries.

An entry is then listed for each model, in the alphabetical order of the model name. At the head of each entry is the model name in bold type, followed by a date or range of dates showing the production period of the instrument. These dates and any other dates in the Reference Listing are naturally as accurate as possible, but must be considered approximate. There exists no foolproof method to pinpoint the exact years of manufacture of most company's instruments, so please bear in mind that the production dates shown throughout the Reference Listing are intended only as a guide.

In italics following the model name and production dates is a brief, one-sentence identification of the bass in question which should help you differentiate that model from others made by the same company.

For some basses there may be a sentence below this, reading 'Similar to … except:'. This will refer to another model entry, and the accompanying description will tell you any major differences between the two.

In most cases there will be a list of specification points next, separated into groups, providing details of the model's features. In the order listed the points may refer to:

Neck, fingerboard, position markers, scale length, frets or fret markers, headstock, tuner arrangement.
Body, finish.
Pickup(s).
Controls, jack location.
Pickguard.
Bridge, tailpiece.
Hardware finish.
Special features (if any).

Some models are made in a number of variations, and where applicable these are listed on separate lines in italics, after the specification points, along with any other general comments.

A few models have only a short entry all in italics. This is usually because the model concerned is a reissue of, or a re-creation based on, an earlier bass. The text will usually refer to the original instrument's entry.

Additional basses made by the company concerned are grouped at the end of each maker's entry under the heading 'Other basses produced include …'. To assist dating of instruments, serial number information where available and/or relevant is given in a separate box.

All this information has been gathered as the result of lengthy and detailed research. The Reference Listing does not pretend to list every bass guitar ever made — that would take a whole shelf of rather tedious books — but is intended to act as a guide to the specifications and production histories of most of the instruments that you will come across on a regular basis. Balafon welcomes any updates to the information shown (our address is given on page 2).

THE BASS BOOK
REFERENCE LISTING

ALEMBIC (USA)

Standard specification features common to all models, unless stated otherwise:
Laminated maple through-neck.
Unbound ebony fingerboard.
Oval position markers.
34in scale, 24 frets.
Truss-rod adjuster at body end.
Metal-key tuners.
Unbound double-cutaway solid body.
Natural finish.
Two pickups.
Controls on body.
Front-mounted jack.
Active circuit.
Four-saddle bridge and separate tailpiece.

Standard Production Models (standard specifications shown)

ELAN 1985-current. *Three controls & mini switch.*
▮ Four-in-line tuners.
▮ Three controls (volume, tone, balance) and tone mini switch.
Various string, scale, style, construction, component and color options.

EPIC 1993-current *Glued-in neck, three controls.*
▮ Glued-in neck; two-a-side tuners; 34in scale.
▮ Three controls (volume, tone, balance).
Various string, scale, construction and color options.

ESSENCE 1991-current *Through-neck, three controls.*
▮ Two-a-side tuners.
▮ Three controls (volume, tone, balance).
Various string, construction and color options.

EUROPA 1986-current *Three controls & three mini switches.*
▮ Four-in-line or two-a-side tuners.
▮ Three controls (volume, tone, balance) and three tone mini switches.
Various string, scale, style, construction and color options.

MARK KING DELUXE 1988-current
Signature on headstock, mahogany & cocobolo body with shallow offset cutaways.
▮ Two-a-side tuners; headstock with Mark King signature.
▮ Four controls (volume, two tone, balance) and two tone mini switches.
Various string, scale, construction and color options.

MARK KING STANDARD 1990-current
Signature on headstock, mahogany & maple or walnut body with shallow offset cutaways.
▮ Two-a-side tuners; headstock with Mark King signature.
▮ Four controls (volume, two tone, balance) and two tone mini switches.
Various string, construction and color options.

SERIES I 1971-current *Center dummy pickup, four controls.*
▮ Two-a-side tuners.
▮ Semi-solid body.
▮ Two pickups plus center hum-canceling unit.
▮ Four controls (two volume, two tone), rotary selector and two mini switches; front-mounted jack and XLR socket; active circuit with outboard power supply.
Various string, scale, style, construction and color options.

SERIES II 1971-current *Center dummy pickup, five controls.*
▮ Two-a-side tuners.
▮ Semi-solid body.
▮ Two pickups plus center hum-canceling unit.
▮ Five controls (three volume, two tone), rotary selector and two rotary switches; front-mounted jack and XLR socket; active circuit with outboard power supply.
Various string, scale, style, construction and color options.

STANLEY CLARKE DELUXE 1988-current
Signature on headstock, mahogany & rosewood body with shallow twin cutaways.
▮ Two-a-side tuners; headstock with Stanley Clarke signature; 30¾in scale, 24 frets.
▮ Four controls (volume, two tone, balance) and two tone mini switches.
Various string, construction and color options.

STANLEY CLARKE STANDARD 1990-current
Signature on headstock, mahogany & maple or walnut body with shallow twin cutaways.
▮ Two-a-side tuners; headstock with Stanley Clarke signature; 30¾in scale, 24 frets.
▮ Four controls (volume, two tone, balance) and two tone mini switches.
Various string, construction and color options.

Other basses produced by Alembic include:

Distillate 1978-90
Persuader 1983-91
Spoiler 1980-94
20th Anniversary 1989

82

Alembic Serial Numbers

The first two digits of the serial number provide the year of manufacture, and these are followed by a letter code indicating the actual model. This precedes the number of the individual instrument which is relevant to total Alembic production.

Model Codes:

AC	– Series I/II (Alembic Canadian Export) 1972-76	
AE	– Series I/II (Alembic Export)	1972-76
AM	– 20th Anniversary	1989
C	– Custom (custom-built bass & guitar)	1971-
D	– Distillate	1978-90
E	– Electrum (guitar)	1978-85
H	– Elan	1985-
J	– Jimmy Johnson Signature	1989-90
JJ	– Jason Newsted Standard	1992-94
JN	– Jason Newsted Deluxe	1991-94
K	– Essence	1991-
M	– Spectrum (guitar)	1992-
MJ	– Mark King Standard	1990-
MK	– Mark King Deluxe	1988-
O	– Orion (guitar)	1994-
P	– Persuader	1983-91
R	– Spoiler (Asian Export – smaller body)	1986-94
S	– Spoiler	1980-94
SC	– Stanley Clarke Deluxe	1988-
SJ	– Stanley Clarke Standard	1990-
U	– Europa	1986-
W	– Epic	1993-
No. only	– Series I (bass & guitar)	1971-
No. only	– Series II (bass & guitar)	1971-

For example: 94H8692 – 1994 Elan, 8692nd instrument produced by Alembic.

AMPEG (USA)

AEB-1 1966-69 *Elongated f-holes through double-cutaway body.*
■ Bolt-on maple neck with ebony fingerboard, dot markers; 34½in scale, 20 frets; truss-rod adjuster at headstock end; full-scroll open 'frame' headstock; two-a-side tuners with rear-facing metal keys.
■ Double-cutaway semi-solid body, full-depth elongated f-holes; sunburst, red, white or blue.
■ Under-bridge pickup.
■ Two controls (volume/on-off, tone) and jack, all on pickguard.
■ Black laminated plastic pickguard.
■ Four-saddle bridge and separate tailpiece.
Also AUB-1 with fretless ebony fingerboard.

ASB-1 1967-69 *Twin thin outward curving horns, triangular holes through body.*
■ Bolt-on maple neck with ebony fingerboard, dot markers; 34½in scale, 20 frets; truss-rod adjuster at headstock end; full-scroll open 'frame' headstock; two-a-side tuners with rear-facing metal keys.
■ Twin-cutaway semi-solid body, thin outward curving horns and full-depth triangular holes; sunburst, red, white or blue.
■ Under-bridge pickup.
■ Two controls (volume/on-off, tone) and jack, all on pickguard.
■ Black laminated plastic pickguard.
■ Four-saddle bridge and separate tailpiece.
Also version with fretless ebony fingerboard.

DAN ARMSTRONG SEE-THROUGH 1969-71 *Clear plexiglass twin-cutaway solid body.*
■ Bolt-on maple neck with rosewood fingerboard, dot markers; 30½in scale, 24 frets; truss-rod adjuster at headstock end; two-a-side tuners with metal keys.
■ Clear plexiglass twin-cutaway solid body.
■ One bar-polepiece pickup.
■ Two controls (volume, tone), two-way selector and jack, all on pickguard.
■ Wood-grain Formica pickguard.
■ Single-saddle bridge/tailpiece.
Also fretless fingerboard version.
Also very small number with black plastic solid body.

Other basses produced by Ampeg include:

AMB-1 semi-solid (c1967-69)
AMUB-1 semi-solid fretless (c1967-69)
SSB short-scale (c1968-69)

ARIA PRO II (Japan)

SB-1000 first version 1979-87 *One pickup, two controls, six-way rotary selector, mini-switch.*
■ Laminated maple through-neck with rosewood fingerboard (ebony from c1982), dot markers; 34in scale, 24 frets; truss-rod adjuster at headstock end; two-a-side tuners with metal keys.
■ Contoured solid body; natural.
■ One plain-top pickup.
■ Two controls (volume, tone), six-way rotary selector and mini switch, all on body; front-mounted jack; active circuit.
■ Four-saddle bridge/tailpiece.

SB-1000 second version 1990-93 *Two pickups, three controls.*
■ Laminated maple through-neck with rosewood fingerboard, dot markers; 34in scale, 24 frets; truss-rod adjuster at headstock end; two-a-side tuners with metal keys.
■ Contoured solid body; black or natural.
■ Two plain-top pickups.

■ Three controls (two volume, one tone); side-mounted jack.
■ Four-saddle bridge/tailpiece.
■ Gold-plated hardware.

SB-1000RI 1994-current *Reissue based on SB-1000 first version.*

Other basses produced by Aria include:

Avante series (introduced 1992)
Integra series (introduced 1986)
Magna series (introduced 1990)
RS series (introduced 1983)
SB series (introduced 1979)

BC RICH

BICH 1979-90 *Large cut-out in lower body bout.*
■ Through-neck with rosewood fingerboard, cloud markers; 30in scale, 24 frets; truss-rod adjuster at headstock end; two-a-side tuners with metal keys.
■ Double-cutaway solid body, large cut-out in lower bout; sunburst, natural or colors.
■ Two split eight-polepiece pickups.
■ Five controls (four volume, one tone), three-way selector, six-way rotary selector, five mini-switches, all on body; side-mounted jack; active circuit.
■ Four-saddle bridge/tailpiece.
Also RICH BICH eight-string with additional four tuners in lower body cut-out (1977-86).
Also RICH BICH LITTLE SISTER (aka SON OF A RICH) four-string with bolt-on neck, dot markers; 22 frets; one split eight-polepiece pickup; volume, tone; four-saddle bridge/tailpiece (1980).

Other basses produced by BC Rich include:

USA

Eagle (introduced 1976)
Mockingbird (introduced 1976)
Warlock (introduced 1981)
Wave (introduced 1981)

JAPAN

NJ series (introduced 1983)

KOREA

Platinum series (introduced 1989)

BURNS (UK)

BISON first version 1962-64 *Single-sided headstock, double-cutaway body with long upward/forward curving horns.*
■ Bolt-on neck with bound ebony fingerboard, dot markers; 33½in scale, 22 frets; truss-rod adjuster at body end; four-in-line tuners with plastic keys.
■ Double-cutaway contoured solid body, long upward/forward curving horns; black, white or custom colors.
■ Three four-polepiece pickups.
■ Two controls (volume, tone), four-way rotary selector, two-way rotary selector and jack, all on pickguard.
■ Black or white laminated plastic pickguard.
■ Four-saddle bridge/tailpiece; string mute.

BISON second version 1964-65 *Two-sided scroll headstock, double-cutaway body with long upward/forward curving horns.*
■ Bolt-on neck with rosewood fingerboard (later bound), dot markers; 33½in scale, 22 frets; truss-rod adjuster at body end; scroll headstock; two-a-side tuners with plastic keys.
■ Double-cutaway solid body, long upward/forward curving horns; black or white.
■ Three plain-top pickups.

■ Three controls (volume, two tone), three-way selector and jack, all on pickguard.
■ Three-piece grey or blue-grey pearl plastic laminated pickguard.
■ Single-saddle bridge/tailpiece; string mute.
■ Three-bar handrest.
Also Baldwin-logo version with two-sided flattened-scroll headstock and metal button tuners (1965-70).

BISON third version 1980-83 *Two-sided headstock, double-cutaway body with long curving horns.*
■ Bolt-on neck with maple fingerboard (rosewood or ebony options), dot markers; 34in scale, 21 frets; truss-rod adjuster at body end; two-a-side tuners with metal keys.
■ Double-cutaway contoured solid body, long curving horns; sunburst or colors.
■ One split eight-polepiece pickup and one straight eight-polepiece pickup.
■ Three controls (volume, two tones), three-way selector and jack, all on pickguard.
■ Four-piece black laminated plastic pickguard.
■ Four-saddle bridge with through-body stringing.

BISON 1994-current *Reissue based on 1964-65 period original.*

Other basses produced by Burns include:

Artiste (1960-62)
Jazz (1964-65)
Nu-Sonic (1964-65)
Shadows (1964-65)
Vista Sonic (1962-64)

CARL THOMPSON (USA)

1974-current *Primarily a custom-order bass builder, but offers a selection of 'standard' models including LES CLAYPOOL SPECIAL in four, five and six-string formats.*

84

DANELECTRO (USA)

LONG HORN model 4423 1958-69 *Twin long outward curving horns.*
▌ Bolt-on neck with rosewood fingerboard, dot markers; 33½ scale, 24 frets; two-a-side tuners with metal or plastic keys.
▌ Twin-cutaway semi-solid body, long outward curving horns; sunburst.
▌ Two pickups.
▌ Two dual-concentric controls (each volume/on-off); side-mounted jack.
▌ Clear plastic pickguard.
▌ Single-saddle bridge/tailpiece.
Also model 4623 with six strings (1958-69).

UB-2 SIX-STRING BASS 1956-59 *Single-cutaway body, two pickups.*
▌ Bolt-on neck with rosewood fingerboard, dot markers; 29½in scale, 24 frets (15 frets from c1957); three-a-side tuners with plastic keys.
▌ Single-cutaway semi-solid body; colors.
▌ Two pickups.
▌ Two dual-concentric controls (each volume/tone) and three-way selector, all on body; side-mounted jack.
▌ Plastic pickguard.
▌ Single-saddle bridge/tailpiece.
Also UB-1 with one pickup; volume, tone and three-way selector.

Other basses produced by Danelectro include:

Short Horn model 3412 (1959-67)
Short Horn model 3612 six-string (1959-67)

EARTHWOOD (USA)

FOUR-STRING ACOUSTIC 1972-73, 1975-79
▌ Maple neck and fingerboard, dot markers; 16 frets; truss-rod adjuster at headstock end; two-a-side tuners with metal keys.

▌ Non-cutaway round soundhole flat-top acoustic; natural.
▌ Single-saddle bridge/tailpiece.

EPIPHONE

RIVOLI EBV-232 1960-70 *Twin cutaway semi, one pickup.*
▌ Glued-in neck with rosewood fingerboard, dot markers; 30½in scale, 20 frets; truss-rod adjuster at headstock end; two-a-side tuners with rear-facing plastic keys (horizontal metal type from c1960).
▌ Bound thinline twin-cutaway semi-acoustic body with two f-holes; sunburst, natural or cherry.
▌ One plastic-cover (metal-cover from 1964) four-polepiece pickup.
▌ Two controls (volume, tone), pushbutton tone switch and jack, all on body.
▌ Black laminated plastic pickguard.
▌ Single-saddle bridge/tailpiece.

Other basses produced by Epiphone include:

USA

Embassy Deluxe (1963-70)
Newport (1961-70)

JAPAN

EA-260 semi-acoustic (1971-76)
ET-285 (1973-76)

KOREA

EBM-4 (1991-current)

Epiphone Serial Numbers

From 1961 to 1970 Epiphone serial numbers are as for Gibson (see later Gibson listing). After 1970 the Epiphone name appeared on basses of oriental origin.

FENDER

Features common to all models, unless stated otherwise:
Bolt-on neck.
Unbound fingerboard.
34in scale, 20 frets.
One string guide on headstock.
Four-in-line tuners.
Metal-key tuners.
Four-screw neckplate.
Unbound, double-cutaway solid body.
Nickel- or chrome-plated hardware.

USA

BASS V 1965-70 *Five strings, 15 frets.*
▌ Maple neck with rosewood fingerboard (bound from c1966, maple fingerboard option c1967), dot markers (blocks from c1966); 34in scale, 15 frets; truss-rod adjuster at body end; five-string headstock, five-in-line tuners.
▌ Offset-waist contoured body; sunburst or colors.
▌ One split black plain-top pickup (unequal halves).
▌ Two controls (volume, tone) and jack, all on metal plate adjoining pickguard.
▌ White or tortoiseshell laminated plastic pickguard.
▌ Five-saddle bridge with through-body stringing.

FENDER CUSTOM SHOP

Limited production basses made by Fender's Custom Shop include an accurate reproduction of the original '51 Precision bass, the 40th Anniversary Precision, plus artist models such as the James Jamerson 'Tribute' Precision & the Jaco Pastorius Jazz, both from 1991 (these last two in limited editions of 100 each).

85

'Standard' Jazz models – chronological order

JAZZ 'pre-CBS' first version 1960-62 *Two eight-polepiece pickups, two dual-concentric controls.*
■ Maple neck with rosewood fingerboard, dot markers; truss-rod adjuster at body end.
■ Offset-waist contoured body; sunburst or colors.
■ Two black eight-polepiece pickups.
■ Two dual-concentric controls (each volume/tone) and jack, all on metal plate adjoining pickguard.
■ White or tortoiseshell laminated plastic pickguard.
■ Four-saddle bridge/tailpiece; body-mounted individual string mutes.

JAZZ 'pre-CBS' second version 1962-65 *Two eight-polepiece pickups, three controls.*
Similar to 'pre-CBS' first version, except:
■ Three controls (two volume, one tone).
■ No body-mounted string mutes.

JAZZ 'CBS' first version 1965-75 *Bound fingerboard.*
Similar to 'pre-CBS' second version, except:
■ Maple neck with bound rosewood fingerboard (bound maple option from c1967), dot markers (blocks from c1966).
■ Body sunburst, natural or colors.

JAZZ 'CBS' second version 1975-81 *'Bullet' truss-rod adjuster at headstock end, three-screw neckplate.*
Similar to 'CBS' first version, except:
■ 'Bullet' truss-rod adjuster at headstock end; three-screw neckplate.
■ White or black laminated plastic pickguard.
Also Antigua version in white/brown shaded finish with matching laminated plastic pickguard (c1977-79).

JAZZ Standard first version 1981-83 *Truss-rod adjuster at body end, white pickups.*

Similar to 'CBS' second version, except:
■ Fretted maple neck, or maple neck with rosewood fingerboard, dot markers; truss-rod adjuster at body end; four-screw neckplate.
■ Pickups white.

JAZZ Standard second version 1983-85 *Controls and jack socket on pickguard.*
Similar to Standard first version, except:
■ Truss-rod adjuster at headstock end.
■ Controls and jack all on pickguard.
■ White plastic pickguard.

JAZZ American Standard 1988-current *22 frets.*
■ Maple neck with rosewood fingerboard, dot markers; 34in scale, 22 frets; truss-rod adjuster at headstock end.
■ Offset-waist contoured body; sunburst or colors.
■ Two black eight-polepiece pickups.
■ Three controls (two volume, one tone) and jack, all on metal plate adjoining pickguard.
■ White laminated plastic pickguard.
■ Four-saddle bridge/tailpiece.

Other Jazz models – A-Z listing

GOLD/GOLD JAZZ 1981-83 *Gold body and hardware.*
Similar to Standard first version (see listing in earlier 'Standard' Jazz models section), except:
■ Body gold.
■ Redesigned heavy-duty four-saddle bridge/tailpiece.
■ Gold-plated hardware.

JAZZ PLUS 1990-current *Controls on body.*
■ Fretted maple neck, or maple neck with rosewood fingerboard, dot markers; 34in-scale, 22 frets; truss-rod adjuster at headstock end.

■ Offset-waist contoured body; sunburst, natural or colors.
■ Two black plain-top pickups.
■ Two dual-concentric controls (volume/balance, treble & bass boost/cut) and rotary selector, all on body; side-mounted jack; active circuit.
■ Four-saddle bridge/tailpiece.

JAZZ PLUS V 1990-current *Five strings, controls on body.*
Similar to Jazz Plus, except:
■ Five-string headstock, five-in-line tuners.
■ Maple neck with rosewood fingerboard only.
■ Five-saddle bridge/tailpiece.

LIMITED EDITION '62 JAZZ 1987-89 *See-through blond body finish, gold-plated hardware.*
Similar to Vintage '62 (see later listing here), except:
■ Body translucent blond.
■ Gold-plated hardware.

VINTAGE '62 JAZZ 1982-current *Reissue based on 1960-62 period original (see 'pre-CBS' first version in earlier 'Standard' Jazz models section).*

MUSTANG 1966-81 *Split pickup, two controls on metal plate adjoining pickguard.*
■ Maple neck with rosewood fingerboard (fretted maple neck option from c1975), dot markers; 30in scale, 19 frets; truss-rod adjuster at body end.
■ Offset-waist contoured body; sunburst, natural or colors, including 'Competition' body stripes option (c1968-72).
■ One split black plain-top pickup.
■ Two controls (volume, tone) and jack, all on metal plate adjoining pickguard.
■ White or pearl or tortoiseshell laminated plastic pickguard (black laminated plastic only from c1975).

■ Four-saddle bridge with through-body stringing; string mutes (1966-c79). *Also Antigua version in white/brown shaded finish with matching laminated plastic pickguard (c1977-79).*

PRECISION first version 1951-57 *Telecaster-style headstock, body-mounted pickup, controls on metal plate adjoining pickguard.*
■ Fretted maple neck, dot markers; truss-rod adjuster at body end.
■ Slab body (contoured from c1954); blond only (or sunburst from c1954, or colors from c1956).
■ One black four-polepiece pickup.
■ Two controls (volume, tone) on metal plate adjoining pickguard; sidemounted jack.
■ Black plastic pickguard (white plastic from c1954).
■ Two-saddle bridge with through-body stringing.

PRECISION second version 1957-81 *Enlarged Stratocaster-style headstock, pickup mounted through pickguard carrying two controls.*
■ Fretted maple neck 1957-c59 and c1969-81, maple neck with rosewood fingerboard c1959-81, maple fingerboard option c1967-69, dot markers; fretless rosewood or maple fingerboard option c1970-81; narrow neck width option c1970-81; truss-rod adjuster at body end.
■ Contoured body; sunbursts, natural or colors.
■ One split black eight-polepiece pickup.
■ Two controls (volume, tone) and jack, all on pickguard.
■ Anodized metal pickguard (white or tortoiseshell laminated plastic from c1959; black laminated plastic from c1975).
■ Four-saddle bridge/tailpiece.
Also slab body version (c1966-67).

Also Antigua version in white/brown shaded finish with matching laminated plastic pickguard (c1977-79).

PRECISION Standard first version 1981-83 *Split white eight-polepiece pickup. Similar to Precision second version, except:*
■ One split white eight-polepiece pickup.
■ White or black laminated plastic pickguard.

PRECISION Standard second version 1983-85 *Truss-rod adjuster at headstock end, split white eight-polepiece pickup. Similar to Standard first version, except:*
■ Truss-rod adjuster at headstock end.
■ White plastic pickguard.

ELITE PRECISION 1983-85 *One split white plain-top pickup.*
■ Fretted maple neck, or maple neck with rosewood fingerboard, dot markers; fretless rosewood fingerboard option; truss-rod adjuster at headstock end.
■ Contoured body; sunburst, natural or colors.
■ One split white plain-top pickup.
■ Two controls (volume, tone) on pickguard; side-mounted jack; active circuit.
■ White laminated plastic pickguard.
■ Four-saddle bridge/tailpiece with individual fine-tuners.
Also 'Gold Elite' version with gold-plated hardware.

ELITE II PRECISION 1983-85 *Two split white plain-top pickups. Similar to Elite, except:*
■ Two split white plain-top pickups.
■ Three controls (two volumes, tone) and two mini switches, all on pickguard.
Also 'Gold Elite II' version with gold-plated hardware.

Also 'Walnut Elite II' version ditto, but with walnut body and neck, ebony fingerboard (also fretless option).

LIMITED EDITION '57 PRECISION 1987-89 *See-through blond body finish, gold-plated hardware. Similar to Vintage '57 (see later listing here), except:*
■ Body translucent blond.
■ Gold-plated hardware.

LIMITED EDITION '62 PRECISION 1987-89 *See-through blond body finish, goldplated hardware. Similar to Vintage '62 (see later listing here), except:*
■ Body translucent blond only.
■ Gold-plated hardware.

PRECISION SPECIAL 1980-83 *"Precision Special" logo on headstock.*
■ Fretted maple neck, or maple neck with rosewood fingerboard, dot markers; truss-rod adjuster at body end.
■ Contoured body; red, blue or white.
■ One split white eight-polepiece pickup.
■ Three controls (volume, two tones), mini switch and jack, all on pickguard; active circuit.
■ White laminated plastic pickguard.
■ Heavy-duty four-saddle bridge/tailpiece.
■ Gold-plated brass hardware.
Also 'Walnut Precision Special' version with fretted walnut neck, walnut body and black laminated plastic pickguard (c1981-83).

US PLUS 1989-92 *One split and one Jazz-type black plain-top pickup.*
■ Fretted maple neck, or maple neck with rosewood fingerboard, dot markers; 34in scale, 22 frets; truss-rod adjuster at headstock end.
■ Contoured body; sunburst, natural or colors.
■ One split black plain-top pickup and one straight black plain-top pickup.

▌ Two controls (volume, tone), three-way selector, push-button switch and jack, all on pickguard.
▌ White laminated plastic pickguard.
▌ Four-saddle bridge/tailpiece with individual fine-tuners.

US PLUS DELUXE 1991-current *One split and one Jazz-type black plain-top pickup, controls on body.*
▌ Fretted maple neck, or maple neck with rosewood fingerboard, dot markers; 34in scale, 22 frets; truss-rod adjuster at headstock end.
▌ Contoured body; sunburst, natural or colors.
▌ One split black plain-top pickup and one straight black plain-top pickup.
▌ Two dual-concentric controls (volume/balance, treble & bass boost/cut) on body; side-mounted jack; active circuit.
▌ Four-saddle bridge/tailpiece with individual fine-tuners.

VINTAGE '57 1982-current *Reissue based on 1957-period original (see second version in earlier 'Standard' Precisions section).*

VINTAGE '62 1982-current *Reissue based on 1962-period original (see second version in earlier 'Standard' Precisions section).*

VI first version 1961-63 *Six strings, VI on headstock, three switches.*
▌ Maple neck with rosewood fingerboard, dot markers; 30in scale, 21 frets; truss-rod adjuster at body end; six-string headstock, six-in-line tuners.
▌ Offset-waist contoured body; sunburst or colors.
▌ Three white six-polepiece pickups, each with flat metal surround.
▌ Two controls (volume, tone) and jack, all on lower metal plate adjoining pickguard; three slide-switches on metal plate inset into pickguard.

▌ White or tortoiseshell laminated plastic pickguard.
▌ Six-saddle bridge; separate vibrato tailpiece.

VI second version 1963-75 *Six strings, VI on headstock, four switches.*
Similar to VI first version, except:
▌ Bound rosewood fingerboard from c1965, dot markers (blocks from c1966).
▌ Body sunburst, natural or colors.
▌ Three white six-polepiece pickups, each with 'sawtooth' metal sides.
▌ Four slide-switches on metal plate inset into pickguard.
▌ Spring-loaded string mute.

Other basses produced by Fender include:

USA

Bullet (1982-83)
Coronado I semi-acoustic (1966-68)
Coronado II semi-acoustic (1967-69)
Coronado Antigua semi-acoustic (1968-71)
Coronado Wildwood semi-acoustic (1967-69)
HM Ultra (1990-91)
Musicmaster (1970-81)
Performer Elite (1985-86)
Telecaster first version (four-polepiece single-coil pickup) (1968-72)
Telecaster special finish versions: Paisley Red or Blue Flower (1968-69)
Telecaster second version (metal-cover humbucker pickup) (1972-78)
Urge Stu Hamm Signature (1992-current)

To remain competitive at all market levels, Fender has sought production facilities in a variety of countries outside the US. These include the following, which are listed together with many of the relevant brands and basses originating from these sources.

INDIA: SUNN by FENDER

Mustang

JAPAN: FENDER

Bullet B30 and B34
HM IV and V
HMT
Jazz Classic '60s reissue
Jazz Contemporary & Contemporary Fretless
Jazz Power Special
Jazz Special and Special Fretless
Jazz Standard and Standard Fretless
Jazz Vintage '60s and Vintage '75
Performer
Precision Acoustic/Electric Fretless
Precision Classic '50s and '60s Reissues
Precision Contemporary
Precision Lyte
Precision Standard 32in and 34in
Precision Vintage '51 and Vintage '75
+ models and variants for domestic market only

JAPAN: HEARTFIELD &/or FENDER:

DR4, DR5 and DR6
DR4C, DR5C and DR6C
Prophecy I, II and III
+ models and variants for domestic market only

JAPAN: SQUIER by FENDER:

Bullet B34
Jazz
Jazz Silver series
Jazz Special Fretless
Jazz Vintage '62
Katana
Precision 32in
Precision Popular
Precision Silver series
Precision Vintage '57 and Vintage '62
+ models and variants for domestic market only

JAPAN: SQUIER (II) by FENDER:

Precision

KOREA: SQUIER by FENDER

HM and HM-V
Jazz Standard
Precision Standard

KOREA: SQUIER (II) by FENDER

Jazz
Precision
Precision Active

MEXICO: FENDER

Jazz
JP-90
Precision
Precision Special (2 pickups)
Prodigy
Urge Stu Hamm Signature Standard

MEXICO: FENDER or SQUIER by FENDER

MB 4 and MB 5

Fender Serial Numbers

Often these merely provide a clue to production date, and should be combined with other aspects, such as construction/component changes, or dated parts, to ensure greater accuracy when trying to determine the age of a bass.

USA number series	Circa	
Up to 6000	1951-54	
Up to 10,000	1954-56	4 or 5 digits (inc 0 or – prefix)
10,000s	1955-56	4 or 5 digits (inc 0 or – prefix)
10,000s to 20,000s	1957	5 or 6 digits (inc 0 or – prefix)
20,000s to 30,000s	1958	5 or 5 digits (inc 0 or – prefix)
30,000s to 40,000s	1959	
40,000s to 50,000s	1960	
50,000s to 70,000s	1961	
60,000s to 90,000s	1962	
80,000sx to 90,000s	1963	
Up to L10,000	1963	L + 5 digits
L10,000s to L20,000s	1963	L + 5 digits
L20,000s to L50,000s	1964	L + 5 digits
L50,000s to L90,000s	1965	L + 5 digits
100,000s	1965	
100,000s to 200,000s	1966-67	
200,000s	1968	
200,000s to 300,000s	1969-70	
300,000s to 500,000s	1973	
400,000s to 500,000s	1974-75	
500,000s to 700,000s	1976	
800,000s to 900,000s	1979-82	
76 or S6 + 5 digits	1976	
S7 or S8 + 5 digits	1977	
S7, S8 or S9 + 5 digits	1978	
S9 or E0 + 5 digits	1979	
S9, E0 or E1 + 5 digits	1980-81	
E1, E2 or E3 + 5 digits	1982	
E2 or E3 + 5 digits	1983	
E3 or E4 + 5 digits	1984-85	
E4 + 5 digits	1987	
E4 or E8 + 5 digits	1988	
E8 or E9 + 5 digits	1989-	
E9 or N9 + 5 digits	1990-	
N0 + 5 digits	1990-	
N1 + 5/6 digits	1991-	
N2 + 5/6 digits	1992-	
N3 + 5/6 digits	1993-	
N4 + 5/6 digits	1994-	

Japan number series	Circa
JV + 5 digits	1982-84
SQ + 5 digits	1983-84
E + 6 digits	1984-87
A + 6 digits	1985-86
B + 6 digits	1985-86
C + 6 digits	1985-86
F + 6 digits	1986-98
G + 6 digits	1987-88
H + 6 digits	1988-89
I + 6 digits	1989-90
J + 6 digits	1989-90
K + 6 digits	1990-91
L + 6 digits	1991-92
M + 6 digits	1992-

These numbers represent the bulk of Fender's American production. There are various anomalies, but as these have no overall dating relevance they are not shown. Also excluded are the series used on Vintage reissues, limited editions and so on; these are specific to certain models and not pertinent to age.

Non-USA manufactured Fenders have their own various number series, which unfortunately do sometimes duplicate the American system. Any confusion has to be resolved by studying other aspects of the instruments to determine correct origins and production dates.

Fender Japan production commenced in 1982 and the company have used a series of prefixes to indicate the year of manufacture. However, this is approximate and, again, should be used as a general guide only.

Fender Japan have confirmed evidence that certain series have been used beyond the production spans listed above, in particular the A-, C- and G-prefixed numbers. This underlines the need for caution when dating by using serial numbers.

FODERA (USA)

1983-current *Models produced include the ANTHONY JACKSON CONTRA BASS, EMPEROR series, IMPERIAL, MARCUS MILLER 5-STRING and MONARCH series.*

FRAMUS (Germany)

STAR 5/150 1959-68 *Single-cutaway semi, two pickups.*
▮ Glued-in neck with bound rosewood fingerboard, dot markers; 20 frets; truss-rod adjuster at headstock end; two-a-side tuners with plastic keys.
▮ Bound thinline pointed (later rounded) single-cutaway semi-acoustic body with two f-holes; sunburst.
▮ Two four-polepiece pickups mounted on metal pickguard (later on body).
▮ Volume and tone controls, rotary selectors (number and layout varies) and jack, all mounted on metal pickguard (later on body).
▮ Single-saddle bridge and separate tailpiece.
Retitled STONE (1966). Also small-body version, with/without f-holes.

Other basses produced by Framus include:

Hollywood 5/148 (introduced 1960)
Nashville (introduced 1975)
Star 5/149 semi-acoustic (introduced 1959)
Strato Deluxe 5/165 (introduced 1964)
Television 5/151 semi-acoustic (introduced 1965)

Framus Serial Numbers

The main number (usually found either on rear of headstock back or label inside body) is followed by a separate pair of digits, accompanied by a letter. The latter two numbers indicate production year.
For example: 51334 63L – 1963
65939 70L – 1970

90

G & L (USA)

L-2000 1980-current *Double-cutaway solid, two pickups, three controls, three mini switches.*
▮ Bolt-on fretted maple neck, later maple neck with maple fingerboard, or maple neck with ebony (later rosewood) fingerboard, dot markers; 34in scale, 21 frets; truss-rod adjuster at headstock end; one string-guide; four-in-line tuners with metal keys; three-screw neckplate.
▮ Contoured double-cutaway solid body; sunburst, natural or colors.
▮ Two eight-polepiece pickups.
▮ Three controls (volume, two tone), three mini switches and jack, all on metal plate (controls and switches later on body with side-mounted jack); active circuit.
▮ Four-saddle bridge/tailpiece.
Early examples without active circuit. Also L-1000 with one pickup, three controls (volume, two tone) and mini switch (1980-93).

Other basses produced by G & L include:

Asat (introduced 1989)
Climax (introduced 1992)
El Toro (introduced 1983)
Lynx (introduced 1985)
SB-2 (introduced 1982)

G&L Serial Numbers

Last number	Date
B000518	1980
B001917	1981
B008525	1982
B010382	1983
B014266	1984
B016108	1985
B017691	1986
B018063	1987
B019627	1988
B020106	1989
B021788	1990
B023013	1991
B024288	1992

GIBSON (USA)

Features common to all models, unless stated otherwise:
Glued-in neck.
Unbound rosewood fingerboard.
Dot markers.
30½in scale, 20 frets.
Truss-rod adjuster at headstock end.
Two-a-side tuners.
Metal-key tuners.
Unbound solid body.
Front-mounted jack.
Nickel- or chrome-plated hardware.

EB 1970 *Two-cutaway beveled-edge body, one pickup, two controls and jack on long pickguard.*
▮ Beveled-edge double-cutaway body; natural.
▮ One metal-cover four-polepiece pickup.
▮ Two controls (volume. tone) and jack, all on pickguard.
▮ Black plastic pickguard.
▮ Single-saddle bridge/tailpiece.

EB-0 first version 1959-61 *Two-cutaway slab body, one pickup.*
▮ Rear-facing plastic tuner keys.
▮ Slab double-cutaway body; red.
▮ One plastic-cover four-polepiece pickup.
▮ Two controls (volume, tone); side-mounted jack.
▮ Black plastic pickguard.
▮ Single-saddle bridge/tailpiece.

EB-0 second version 1961-74 *Two-cutaway beveled-edge body, one pickup.*
▮ Beveled-edge double-cutaway body; red, brown, natural or black.
▮ One plastic cover (metal-cover from c1962) four-polepiece pickup.
▮ Two controls (volume, tone).
▮ Black laminated plastic pickguard.
▮ Single-saddle bridge/tailpiece.
Also EB-0L with 34½in scale (c1970-74).

Also EB-0F with built-in active fuzz circuit and controls (1962-65).
Also EB-6 second version with six strings and pushbutton tone switch (1961-62).

EB-1 1969-71 *Violin shape body, one metal-cover pickup.*
Similar to ELECTRIC BASS, except:
■ Horizontal metal tuner buttons.
■ One metal-cover four-polepiece pickup.
See later ELECTRIC BASS listing.

EB-2 1958-61, 1964-70 *Twin-cutaway semi, one pickup.*
■ Two-a-side tuners with rear-facing plastic keys (horizontal metal type from c1960).
■ Bound thinline twin-cutaway semi-acoustic body with two f-holes; sunburst, natural or colors.
■ One plastic-cover (metal-cover from 1964) four-polepiece pickup.
■ Two controls (volume, tone) plus pushbutton tone switch (from c1959).
■ Black laminated plastic pickguard.
■ Single-saddle bridge/tailpiece.
Also EB-2D with two pickups (1966-72).
Also EB-6 first version, with six strings (1959-61).

EB-3 1961-79 *Two-cutaway beveled-edge body, two pickups.*
■ Rosewood fingerboard (bound c1969-72); 30½in scale, 20 frets (some with 19 or 21 frets from c1969); slotted headstock c1969-72.
■ Beveled-edge double-cutaway body; red, brown, natural or white.
■ One plastic-cover (metal-cover from c1962) four-polepiece pickup plus smaller metal-cover four-polepiece pickup.
■ Four controls (two volume, two tone) and four-way rotary selector.
■ Black laminated plastic pickguard.
■ Single-saddle bridge/tailpiece (four-saddle bridge/tailpiece from c1974).
Also EB-3L with 34½in scale (c1970-74).
Also EB-6 third version with six strings and three-way selector (1962-65).

EB-4L 1972-73 *Two-cutaway beveled-edge body, one pickup, three-way tone selector.*
■ 34½in scale, 20 frets.
■ Beveled-edge double-cutaway body; red or brown.
■ One metal-cover four-polepiece pickup.
■ Two controls (volume, tone) and three-way tone selector.
■ Black laminated plastic pickguard.
■ Single-saddle bridge/tailpiece.

EB-6 *Three versions, see earlier EB-O, EB-2 and EB-3 listings.*

ELECTRIC BASS 1953-58 *Violin shape body.*
■ Two-a-side tuners with rear facing plastic keys.
■ Carved-top violin shape body with or without painted f-holes; brown.
■ One plastic-cover four-polepiece pickup.
■ Two controls (volume, tone); side-mounted jack.
■ Brown plastic pickguard.
■ Single-saddle bridge/tailpiece.
■ Optional extendable endpin.
Officially retitled EB-1 in 1958.
Reissued as EB-1 1969-71, see earlier listing.

LES PAUL 1969-70 *24 frets, single-cutaway body, dot markers.*
■ Rosewood fingerboard, dot markers; 30½in scale, 24 frets.
■ Bound carved-top single-cutaway body; brown.
■ Two round-end plastic-cover pickups.
■ Three controls (volume, bass, treble) plus three-way selector, all on body; phase slide switch and tone selector, both on small panel.
■ Single-saddle bridge/tailpiece.

LES PAUL TRIUMPH 1971-79 *24 frets, single-cutaway body, block markers.*
■ Bound rosewood fingerboard, block markers; 30½in scale, 24 frets.
■ Bound carved-top single-cutaway body; brown or white.

■ Two round-end plastic cover pickups.
■ Three controls (volume, bass, treble) plus three-way selector, phase slide switch, tone selector, impedance slide switch, and jack, all on black laminated plastic panel.
■ Four-saddle bridge/tailpiece.

THUNDERBIRD II first version (reverse) 1963-65 *Through-neck, offset body with longer right horn, one pickup.*
■ Through-neck; 34½in scale, 20 frets; four-in-line tuners.
■ Reversed-offset body with raised through-neck center section; sunburst or colors.
■ One metal-cover plain-top pickup.
■ Two controls (volume, tone).
■ White laminated plastic pickguard with stylised bird emblem.
■ Four-saddle bridge and separate tailpiece.

THUNDERBIRD II second version (non-reverse) 1965-69 *Glued-in neck, double-cutaway body with shallow rounded horns, one pickup.*
■ Glued-in neck; 34½in scale, 20 frets; four-in-line tuners.
■ Double-cutaway body; sunburst or colors.
■ One metal-cover plain-top pickup.
■ Two controls (volume, tone).
■ White laminated plastic pickguard with stylized bird emblem.
■ Four-saddle bridge and separate tailpiece.

THUNDERBIRD II 1983-84 *Reissue based on 1963-65 period original (see earlier listing).*

THUNDERBIRD IV first version (reverse) 1963-65 *Through-neck, offset body with longer right horn, two pickups.*
Similar to Thunderbird II first version, except:
■ Two metal-cover plain-top pickups.
■ Three controls (two volumes, one tone).

91

THUNDERBIRD IV second version (non-reverse) 1965-69 *Glued-in neck, double-cutaway body with shallow rounded horns, two pickups.*
Similar to Thunderbird II second version, except:
■ Two metal-cover plain-top pickups.
■ Three controls (two volumes, one tone).

THUNDERBIRD IV third version (reverse) 1987-current *Black pickups, black plated hardware.*
Similar to Thunderbird IV first version, except:
■ Ebony fingerboard.
■ Two black-cover plain-top pickups with no surrounds.
■ Four-saddle bridge/tailpiece.
■ Black-plated hardware.

THUNDERBIRD 76 1976-77
Red/white/blue bird emblem, four-saddle bridge/tailpiece.
Similar to Thunderbird IV first version, except:
■ Sunburst, natural or colors.
■ US Bicentennial red/white/blue stylized bird emblem.
■ Four-saddle bridge/tailpiece.

THUNDERBIRD 79 1979 *Four-saddle bridge/tailpiece.*
Similar to Thunderbird IV first version, except:
■ Sunburst, natural or black.
■ Four-saddle bridge/tailpiece.

TRIUMPH BASS *See earlier LES PAUL TRIUMPH listing.*

Other basses produced by Gibson include:

EB-650 semi-acoustic (1992-current)
EB-750 semi-acoustic (1992-current)
Explorer (1984-87)
Flying V (1981-82)
Grabber / G-1 (1974-82)
G-3 (1975-82)
L-9S / Ripper (1973-82)

Les Paul Signature (1973-79)
LPB Les Paul series (1992-current)
Melody Maker (1968-70)
Q-80 / Q-90 Combo (1986-92)
RD Artist (1977-82)
RD Standard (1977-79)
SB 300 & 400 (1971-72)
SB 350 & 450 (1972-74)
Victory Artist (1981-86)
Victory Custom (1982-84)
Victory Standard (1981-87)
IV (1987-89)
V (1987-89)
20/20 (1987-89)

92

Gibson Serial Numbers

Gibson have adopted various numbering systems over the past 40 years and, while some can provide a very accurate indication of production date, others merely serve to confuse courtesy of minimal logic, chronological irrelevance and inconsistent duplication. In such instances other age related clues must suffice to deduce approximate vintage.

From 1953 to 1960 the serial number comprised a five-digit number, ink-stamped on to the rear of the headstock. The first digit was slightly apart from the other four and signified the year of manufacture. In 1955 increased output necessitated the addition of a sixth digit (located after the date code) to some sequences. In both styles, the first digit provides the date:

3 = 1953	7 = 1957
4 = 1954	8 = 1958
5 = 1955	9 = 1959
6 = 1956	0 = 1960

During 1961 inked-on numbering was replaced by a method using digits actually stamped into the back of the headstock. At this time Gibson introduced a new serialization system for all instruments. These numbers were supposed to be allocated in a strict sequence, but this didn't happen in practice and many duplications occur.

Number series	Circa
100 to 61,000s	1961-62
61,000s to 70,000s	1962-64
71,000s to 99,000s	1962-63
000,000s	1967, 73-75
100,000s	1963-67, 70-75
100,000s to 144,000s	1963-64, 67
147,00s to 199,000s	1963-65
200,000s to 290,000s	1964-65, 73-75
300,000s	1965-68, 74-75
301,000s to 305,000s	1965
306,000s to 307,000s	1965,67
309,0900s to 310,000s	1965, 67
311,000s to 326,000s	1965, 67
328,000s to 329,000s	1965
329,000s to 332,000s	1965, 67-68
332,000s to 368,000s	1965-66
368,000s to 370,000s	1966-67
380,000s to 385,000s	1966
390,000s	1967

Number series	Circa
400,000s	1965-68, 74-75
401,000s to 409,000s	1966
420,000s to 438,000s	1966
500,000s	1965-66, 68-69, 74-75
501,000s to 503,000s	1965
501,000s to 530,000s	1968
530,000s	1966
530,000s to 545,000s	1969
540,000s	1966
550,000s to 556,000s	1966
558,000s to 567,000s	1969
570,000s	1966
580,000s	1969
600,000s	1966-69, 70-72, 74-75
601,000s	1969
605,000s to 606,000s	1969
700,000s	1966-67, 70-72
750,000s	1968-69
800,000s	1966-69, 73-75
801,000s to 812,000s	1966, 69
812,000s to 814,000s	1969
817,000s to 819,000s	1969
820,000s	1969
820,000s to 823,000s	1966
824,000s	1969
828,000s to 847,000s	1966, 69
847,000s to 858,000s	1966
859,000s to 880,000s	1967
893,000s to 897,000s	1967
895,000s to 896,000s	1968
897,000s to 898,000s	1967
899,000s to 920,000s	1968
900,000s	1968, 70-72
940,00s to 943,000s	1968
945,000s	1968
947,000s to 966,000s	1968
970,000s to 972,000s	1968

In 1975, Gibson at last replaced their previous haphazard system with a much simpler scheme, which ran for three years. This used eight digits, the first two of which formed a coded date prefix: 99 = 1975; 00 = 1976; 06 = 1977. And instead of being stamped into the back of the headstock, serial numbers from this series were part of a decal which also included the model name and 'Made in USA'.

In 1977 Gibson reverted to stamping the serial number into the rear of the headstock, and changed the serial number system yet again. The number remained at eight digits, but now the first and fifth indicated the year of production. For example, 93291369 indicates a model produced in 1991. This system has proved to be successful and reliable, and is still in operation at the time of writing.

6070 1962-72 *Twin-cutaway semi, one pickup.*
▌ Glued-in neck with ebony fingerboard, dot markers; 34in scale, 20 frets; truss-rod adjuster at headstock end; two-a-side tuners with metal keys.
▌ Bound thinline twin-cutaway semi-acoustic body with two painted f-holes; sunburst or natural.
▌ One pickup.
▌ One control (volume) and on-off switch, both on body; side-mounted jack.
▌ Four-saddle bridge and separate tailpiece.
▌ Extendable endpin (not fitted from c1964).
Also 6072 with two pickups, three controls and three switches (1967-72).

Other basses produced by Gretsch include:

Bikini (1961)
6071 semi-acoustic (1965-72)
6073 semi-acoustic (1965-72)
7615 (1972-74)
7627 TK-300 (1977-81)
7629 Committee (1977-81)

Gretsch Serial Numbers

Gretsch serial numbering is not consistent enough to provide any more than a guide to actual production date.

1960-65

34000s-39000s	1960
39000s-45000s	1961
46000s-52000s	1962
53000s-63000s	1963
63000s-77000s	1964
77000s-85000s	1965

1965-72

First, or first two, digits indicate month (1-12), next number shows last digit of year (196 5 – 197 2), remaining characters are not applicable.
For example : 96220 – September 1966.

1973-81

The system is as before, but there is sometimes a hyphen between the month indicator digit/s and the year number.
For example : 5-5125 – May 1975.

93

GUILD (USA)

ASHBORY BASS 1987-89 *Angled headstock and minute body.*
▌ Wood one-piece neck/body; dot markers; 18in scale, 24 fret markers; four-in-line locking tuners; colors.
▌ One under-bridge pickup.
▌ Three controls (volume, two tone) and mini switch, all on body; sidemounted jack; active circuit.
▌ Single-saddle bridge/tailpiece.
Also Ashbory UK-made original version, similar to Guild (1986-87).
Also Ashbory UK-made revised version with two-sided headstock and larger straight-sided body (1989-current).

GUILD STARFIRE I 1964-75 *Twin-cutaway semi, one pickup.*
■ Glued-in neck with rosewood fingerboard, dot markers; fretless option; 30½in scale, 21 frets; truss-rod adjuster at headstock end; two-a-side tuners with plastic or metal keys.
■ Bound thinline twin-cutaway semi-acoustic body with two f-holes; sunburst or red.
■ One four-polepiece pickup.
■ Two controls (volume, tone) on body; side-mounted jack.
■ Four-saddle bridge/tailpiece.
Also STARFIRE II with two pickups, five controls (three volume, two tone), plus three-way and two-way selectors (1967-77).

B-301/302 (introduced 1977)
Jet-Star (introduced 1964)
JS-II (introduced 1971)
M-85-II Bluesbird (introduced 1967)
SB-602 Pilot (introduced 1985)

94

HAGSTROM (Sweden)

H8 1967-69 *Eight strings.*
■ Bolt-on maple neck with bound rosewood fingerboard, dot markers; 21 frets; truss-rod adjuster at body end; one string-guide; two-a-side tuners with metal keys; four-screw neckplate.
■ Contoured double-cutaway solid body; sunburst or red.
■ Two four-polepiece pickups.
■ One control (volume) and five slide-switches, all on pickguard; front-mounted jack.
■ Eight-saddle bridge/tailpiece.

Other basses produced by Hagstrom include:
Coronado IV (introduced 1964)
EBP26 (introduced 1959)

H-IIB (introduced 1965)
Scanbass (introduced 1978)
Swede (introduced 1971)

HAMER

12-STRING 1980-current *12 strings.*
■ Glued-in neck with rosewood fingerboard, dot markers; 30½in scale, 21 frets; truss-rod adjuster at headstock end; six-a-side tuners with metal keys (four large, eight small).
■ Double-cutaway solid body; sunburst or colors.
■ Two pickups.
■ Three controls (two volume, one tone); side-mounted jack; active circuit.
■ Eight-saddle bridge and separate tailpiece.
Also eight-string version.
Also 34in scale version.

Other basses produced by Hamer include:

USA

Chaparral (introduced 1986)
Cruisebass (introduced 1982)
Impact (introduced 1990)

KOREA

Centaura (introduced 1994)
Chaparral (introduced 1993)

HARMONY

H-22 1962-69 *Single-cutaway thinline semi, one pickup.*
■ Bolt-on neck with rosewood fingerboard, dot markers; 30in scale, 20 frets; truss-rod adjuster at headstock end; two-a-side tuners with plastic keys.
■ Bound thinline single-cutaway semi-acoustic body, two f-holes; sunburst.
■ One pickup.
■ Two controls (volume, tone) and tone selector; side-mounted jack.

■ White plastic pickguard.
■ Single-saddle bridge and separate tailpiece.
Became H-22/1 with twin-cutaway body from 1969.

Other basses produced by Harmony include:

USA

H-25 (introduced 1966)
H-27 semi-acoustic (introduced 1966)
H-420 semi-acoustic (introduced 1972)
H-426 (introduced 1972)

KOREA

H-8100 (introduced 1980)

HÖFNER (Germany)

500/1 1956-current *Violin shape semi.*
■ Glued-in neck with rosewood fingerboard (later bound), dot markers; 30in scale, 22 frets; truss-rod adjuster at headstock end; two-a-side tuners with plastic keys.
■ Bound violin shape semi-acoustic body, no f-holes; sunburst.
■ Two pickups.
■ Two controls (volume) and three slide-switches, all on plastic plate; side-mounted jack.
■ Tortoiseshell plastic (later white pearl plastic) pickguard.
■ Four-saddle bridge and separate tailpiece.
Also 500/1B and 500/1M, both with active circuits.
Also 500/1 CAVERN reissue based on 1961-period original.
Also 500/1 VINTAGE '63 reissue based on 1963-period original.
Also 5000/1 with bound ebony fingerboard, twin-dot markers; natural finish; gold-plated hardware. Available with active circuit (this version also known as the G500/1 SUPER BEATLE).

Other basses produced by Höfner include:

188 six-string (introduced 1963)
500/2 semi-acoustic (introduced 1965)
500/3 semi-acoustic known as Senator in UK (introduced 1960)
500/5 semi-acoustic known as President in UK (introduced 1957)
500/7 semi-acoustic known as Verithin in UK (introduced 1963)

IBANEZ (Japan)

MUSICIAN MC-900 *1979 Through-neck solid, two pickups, five controls, three-way select and mini switch.*
▌ Laminated maple through-neck with ebony fingerboard, dot markers; 34in scale, 22 frets; truss-rod adjuster at headstock; two-a-side tuners with metal keys.
▌ Contoured double-cutaway solid body; natural.
▌ Two pickups.
▌ Five controls (volume, four tone), three-way selector, mini switch and jack, all on body; active circuit.
▌ Four-saddle bridge/tailpiece.
Replaced by MC-924 in late-1979.

Other basses produced by Ibanez include:

Musician series (introduced 1979)
Roadstar series (introduced 1982)
Roadster series (introduced 1979)
Soundgear series (introduced 1988)
Studio series (introduced 1979)

JAYDEE (UK)

SUPERNATURAL CLASSIC *1980-current Body with shallow indents forming point on lower bout.*
▌ Laminated maple through-neck with bound ebony fingerboard, dot markers; 34in scale, 21 frets; truss-rod adjuster at headstock end; two-a-side tuners with metal keys.

▌ Contoured double-cutaway solid body; natural or colors.
▌ Two wood-cover pickups.
▌ Five controls (volume, four tone), four-way rotary selector, mini switch, jack and XLR socket, all on body; active circuit.
▌ Four-saddle bridge and two separate tailpieces.
Also pre-production examples from 1978.

Other basses in the Supernatural series include:

Calibas, Celeste, GA 24, Mark King, Roadie, Session, Supersession, Studio and Video.

KEN SMITH (USA)

BT CUSTOM VI *1980-current Body with small point on slightly offset lower bout.*
▌ Laminated maple through-neck with ebony fingerboard, dot markers; 34in scale, 24 frets; truss-rod adjuster at headstock end; three-a-side tuners with metal keys.
▌ Double cutaway solid body; natural or colors.
▌ Two pickups.
▌ Three controls (volume, balance, treble/ bass dual-concentric) all on body; side-mounted jack; active circuit.
▌ Six-saddle bridge/tailpiece.
Also four-string and five-string versions.

Other basses produced by Ken Smith include:

BT series (1980-current)
BMT Elite series (1992-current)
Burner series (1989-current)
CR series (1991-current)
SEB-II (1979-85)

KRAMER (USA)

650B ARTIST *1976-79 Aluminum neck with twin-prong headstock, crown fingerboard markers.*

▌ Bolt-on aluminiun neck with synthetic fingerboard, crown markers; 33¾in scale, 20 frets; twin-prong headstock, two-a-side tuners with metal keys.
▌ Double-cutaway laminated solid body; natural.
▌ Two plain-top pickups.
▌ Four controls (two volume, two tone) and three-way selector, all on body; side-mounted jack.
▌ Four-saddle bridge/tailpiece.

FERRINGTON I *1986-89 Double-cutaway electro-acoustic, asymmetric soundhole.*
▌ Bolt-on maple neck with bound rosewood fingerboard, diamond markers; 22 frets; truss-rod adjuster at headstock end; four-in-line tuners with metal keys; four-screw neckplate.
▌ Bound double-cutaway flat-top acoustic body with asymmetric soundhole; sunburst or colors.
▌ Under-bridge pickup.
▌ Three controls (volume, two tone) and jack, all on body side; active circuit.
▌ Four-saddle bridge/tailpiece.

Other basses produced by Kramer include:

DMZ Custom series (introduced 1978)
Pioneer series (introduced 1984)
Stagemaster series (introduced 1981)
XL series (introduced 1980)
250B, 350B and 450B (introduced 1976)

KUBICKI (USA)

EX-FACTOR *1985-current Headless design with fingerboard extension clamp mechanism for bottom string.*
▌ Headless bolt-on maple neck with ebony fingerboard; 32in scale (36in with extension), 23 frets (25 with extension); truss-rod adjuster at 'headstock' end.
▌ Contoured double-cutaway solid body; colors.
▌ Two pickups.

▌Two dual-concentric controls (volume/balance, treble/bass) and six-way rotary selector, all on body; side-mounted jack; active circuit.
▌Four-saddle bridge/tuner-tailpiece.
Also 34in scale, 24 frets option.
34in scale fretless fingerboard option.

Other basses produced by Kubicki include:

Factor 4 (1985-current)
Key Factor 4 and 5 (1994-current)

MARTIN (USA)

B-65 1989-current. *Non-cutaway acoustic-electric, tortoiseshell binding and pickguard.*
▌Glued-in neck with ebony fingerboard; 34in scale, 23 frets; truss-rod adjuster at body end; two-a-side tuners with metal keys.
▌Non-cutaway flat-top acoustic body, round soundhole; natural.
▌Under-bridge pickup.
▌Two controls (volume, tone) and jack, all side-mounted.
▌Single-saddle bridge/tailpiece.
Also B-40 with white binding; black pickguard (1989-current).
Also BC-40 with single-cutaway body, oval soundhole (1992-current).
Also B5-40 with five strings (1992-current).

MODULUS GRAPHITE (USA)

QUANTUM SIX-STRING 1983-current
Double-cutaway body with long curving horns.
▌Graphite through-neck with synthetic fingerboard, dot markers; 35in scale, 24 frets; three-a-side tuners with metal keys.
▌Contoured double-cutaway wood solid body; natural or colors.
▌Two pickups.

▌Four controls (volume, two-tone, balance).
▌Six-saddle bridge/tailpiece.
Also four-string and five-string versions.
Also numerous options and custom variations.

Other basses by Modulus Graphite include:

Bassstar series (introduced 1981)
M92 series (introduced 1992)
Quantum series (introduced 1983)

MUSIC MAN (USA)

Features common to all models, unless stated otherwise:
Bolt-on neck.
Unbound fingerboard.
Dot markers.
34in scale, 21 frets.
'Three-and-one' tuner arrangement.
Metal-key tuners.
Unbound, double-cutaway solid body.
Active circuit.
Nickel- or chrome-plated hardware.

Music Man 1976-84

CUTLASS 1983 *Black neck. Cutlass I similar to StingRay, II similar to Sabre, except:*
▌Black carbon graphite neck.

SABRE 1978-84 *Two pickups.*
▌Fretted maple neck (narrow width option), or maple neck with rosewood fingerboard; fretless ebony fingerboard option; truss-rod adjuster at headstock end; one string-guide (on G & D strings); three-screw neckplate (four-screw from 1980).
▌Contoured body; sunburst, natural or colors.
▌Two eight-polepiece pickups.
▌Three controls (volume, two tone), three-way selector, two mini switches and jack, all on metal plate adjoining pickguard.
▌Black or white laminated plastic pickguard.
▌Four-saddle bridge/tailpiece; individual string mutes.

STINGRAY 1976-84 *One pickup.*
▌Fretted maple neck (narrow width option), or maple neck with rosewood fingerboard; fretless ebony fingerboard option; truss-rod adjuster at headstock end; one string-guide (on G & D strings); three-screw neckplate (four-screw from 1980).
▌Slab body; sunburst, natural or colors.
▌One eight-polepiece pickup.

96

■ Three controls (volume, two tone) and jack, all on metal plate.
■ Black or white laminated plastic pickguard.
■ Four-saddle bridge with (until 1980) through-body stringing; individual string mutes.

Ernie Ball Music Man 1984-current

SABRE 1984-91 *Two pickups.*
■ Fretted maple neck (later maple neck with maple fingerboard) or maple neck with rosewood fingerboard; fretless rosewood fingerboard option (later pau ferro); truss-rod adjuster at headstock end (later at body end); one string-guide (on D & A strings); four-screw neckplate.
■ Contoured body; sunburst, natural or colors.
■ Two plain-top pickups.
■ Three controls (volume, two tone), five-way selector and jack, all on metal plate adjoining pickguard.
■ Clear, black, black laminated or white laminated plastic pickguard.
■ Four-saddle bridge/tailpiece; individual string mutes.

STINGRAY 1984-current *21 frets, one pickup.*
■ Fretted maple neck (later maple neck with maple fingerboard) or maple neck with rosewood fingerboard; fretless rosewood fingerboard option (later pau ferro); truss-rod adjuster at headstock end (later at body end); one string-guide (on D & A strings); four-screw neckplate (later six-screw).
■ Contoured body; sunburst, natural or colors.
■ One eight-polepiece pickup.
■ Three controls (volume, two tone) and jack, all on metal plate.
■ Clear, black, black laminated or white laminated plastic pickguard.
■ Four-saddle bridge/tailpiece; individual string mutes.

Also four control option (volume, three tone), with side-mounted jack.

STINGRAY 5 1988-current *Five strings, one pickup.*
■ Maple neck with maple or rosewood fingerboard; fretless rosewood fingerboard option (later pau ferro); 34in scale, 22 frets; truss rod adjuster at body end; one string guide; five-string headstock, four-and-one tuners; six-screw neckplate.
■ Contoured body; sunburst, natural or colors.
■ One eight-polepiece pickup.
■ Four controls (volume, three tone) and three-way selector, all on pickguard; side-mounted jack.
■ Black or white laminated plastic pickguard.
■ Five-saddle bridge/tailpiece.

Other basses by Ernie Ball Music Man include:

Silhouette six-string (1992-current)
Sterling (1994-current)

Music Man Serial Numbers

The serial numbers found on 'pre-Ernie Ball' examples give no indication of production date, but such information can usually be found on the body end of the neck. Ernie Ball Music Man instruments make life much easier – they employ a numbering system that indicates the year via the first two digits.

For example: 91818 – 1991

OVATION (USA/KOREA)

ELITE 5 1994-current *Single-cutaway electro-acoustic, ornate multi-soundhole.*
■ Glued-in neck with bound ebony fingerboard, propeller markers; 34in scale, 24 frets; truss-rod adjuster at body end; two-a-side tuners with metal keys.
■ Single-cutaway wood top/synthetic bowl-back acoustic body, multi-sound hole; sunburst, natural or black.
■ Under-bridge pickup.
■ One control (volume) and three sliders (tone); side-mounted jack; active circuit.
■ Single-saddle bridge/tailpiece.
Also Elite 4 with four strings (1991-current).

Other basses produced by Ovation include:

Applause series electro (1990-current)
Celebrity series electro (1992-current)
Magnum I/II (1976-79)
Magnum III/IV (1980-83)
Typhoon series semi acoustic (1968-71)

OVERWATER (UK)

C BASS 1985-86 *Double-cutaway body with offset waist and lower bout.*
■ Through-neck with bound ebony fingerboard, diamond markers; 36in scale, 24 frets; truss-rod adjuster at headstock end; four-in-line tuners with metal keys.
■ Double-cutaway solid body, offset waist and lower bout; sunburst, natural or colors.
■ Two pickups.
■ Four controls (volume, two tone, balance) all on body; side-mounted jack; active circuit.
■ Four-saddle bridge/tailpiece.
Also various custom options.

Other basses by Overwater include:

Artisan series (introduced 1986)
Fusion series (introduced 1990)
Original series (introduced 1978)
Progress series (introduced 1988)
Progress II series (introduced 1990)

PEAVEY (USA)

MIDIBASE 1992-94 *Digital display on side of left horn.*
▮ Bolt-on maple neck with rosewood fingerboard, dot markers; 34in scale, 21 frets; truss-rod adjuster at headstock end; four-in-line tuners with metal keys; four-screw neckplate.
▮ Contoured double-cutaway solid body; white.
▮ Two pickups; four MIDI pickups in bridgeplate.
▮ Four controls (volume, MIDI volume, tone, balance) and mini switch, all on body; side-mounted jack and MIDI socket; active circuit.
▮ Four-saddle/four-section bridge/tailpiece.
Replaced by CYBERBASS with 22 frets; redesigned headstock and body; two dual-concentric controls and mini switch; grey pearl laminated plastic pickguard; redesigned bridge/tailpiece (1994-current).

Other bases produced by Peavey include:

Dyna-Bass (introduced 1985)
Palaedium (introduced 1991)
RJ IV (introduced 1991)
TL series (introduced 1989)
T-40 (introduced 1977)

PEDULLA (USA)

PENTABUZZ 1976-current *Double-cutaway body with bulbous horns.*
▮ Laminated maple through-neck with fretless ebony fingerboard, dot markers; 34in scale, 24 fret markers; truss-rod adjuster at headstock; 'three-and-two' tuner arrangement.
▮ Contoured double-cutaway solid body; sunburst, natural or colors.
▮ One split pickup and one straight pickup, or two straight pickups.
▮ Four controls (three volume, one tone) three-way selector and mini switch, all

on body; side-mounted jack; active circuit.
▮ Five-saddle bridge/tailpiece.
Also BUZZ four-string, HEXABUZZ six-string and OCTABUZZ eight-string fretless versions.
Also MVP four-, five-, six- and eight-string fretted versions.

Other basses produced by M.V. Pedulla include:

Exotic series (introduced 1992)
Mark Egan Signature series (introduced 1992)
Series II series (introduced 1988)
Thunderbass series (introduced 1992)
Thunderbolt series (introduced 1994)

RICKENBACKER (USA)

Features common to all models, unless stated otherwise:
Through-neck.
33½in scale, 20 frets.
Truss-rod adjuster at headstock end.
Two-sided headstock with hooked 'cresting wave' top, two-a-side tuners.
Metal-key tuners.
Solid body featuring offset cutaways, with hooked long left horn providing a 'high cresting wave' profile across both.
Two pickups.
Four controls (two volume, two tone) and three-way selector, all on pickguard.
Side-mounted jack/s.
Four-saddle bridge/tailpiece.
Nickel- or chrome-plated hardware, also black-plated option.

4000 1957-84 *One pickup*
▮ Unbound rosewood fingerboard, dot markers.
▮ Unbound body; sunburst, natural or colors.
▮ One pickup.
▮ Two controls (volume, tone).
▮ Gold plastic pickguard (or white plastic from c1958; white only from c1963, later black plastic option).
Also 4000FL fretless version.

4001 1961-86 *Triangle markers, two pickups.*
▮ Bound rosewood fingerboard, triangle markers.
▮ Bound body; sunburst, natural or colors.
▮ White plastic pickguard (later black plastic option).
Also 4001FL fretless version.

4001CS CHRIS SQUIRE 1991-current
Signature on pickguard
Similar to 1960s period 4001S (see later listing), except:
▮ Custom-shape neck; padauk fingerboard.

■ Cream finish only.
■ Chris Squire signature and 'Limited Edition' on pickguard.

4001S 1961-69, 1980-84 *Dot markers, two pickups.*
■ Unbound rosewood fingerboard, dot markers.
■ Unbound body; sunburst, natural or colors.

■ White plastic pickguard (later black plastic option).
Known as Model 1999 in UK (1964-69).
Also 4001SF fretless version.

4001V63 1985-current
Reissue based on 1963-period 4001S (see earlier listing).

4002 1976-85 *Two pickups on restyled black pickguard.*
■ Bound ebony fingerboard, dot markers; 33½in scale, 21 frets.
■ Bound body; sunburst or natural.
■ Three side-mounted jacks (mono, stereo, low impedance).
■ Restyled black laminated plastic pickguard.

4003 first version 1979-84 *Triangle markers, two pickups, two-piece pickguard.*
■ Bound rosewood fingerboard, triangle markers; truss-rod adjuster at body end.
■ Bound body; sunburst, natural or colors.
■ White or black plastic two-piece pickguard.
Also 4003FL fretless version.

4003 second version 1984-current *Triangle markers, two pickups.*
Similar to 4003 first version, except:
■ Truss-rod adjuster at headstock end.
■ One-piece pickguard.
Also 4003FL fretless version.

4003S first version 1981-84 *Dot markers, two pickups, two-piece pickguard.*
■ Unbound rosewood fingerboard, dot markers; truss-rod adjuster at body end.
■ Unbound body; sunburst, natural or colors.
■ White or black plastic two-piece pickguard.

4003S second version 1984-current *Dot markers, two pickups.*
Similar to 4003S first version, except:
■ Truss-rod adjuster at headstock end.
■ One-piece pickguard.
Also 4003S TUXEDO with white neck, fingerboard and body; black pickguard and black-plated hardware (1987).
Also 4003S/SPC BLACKSTAR with black fingerboard and black-plated hardware (1989).

Rickenbacker Serial Numbers

Since 1960 the Rickenbacker company has employed a numbering system that is considered to provide an accurate guide to the year of manufacture.
From 1961 to 1986 two, three or four digit numbers were used, always partnered by a two letter coded prefix. The first letter indicated the year while the second signified the month.
In 1987 a new scheme was introduced that is still in operation. It uses two, three or four digit numbers as before, but now the coded prefix consists of a letter and a number. The letter denotes the month as before, while the single number provides the year.

1961-1986
First letter = Year

A	– 1961	N	– 1974
B	– 1962	O	– 1975
C	– 1963	P	– 1976
D	– 1964	Q	– 1977
E	– 1965	R	– 1978
F	– 1966	S	– 1979
G	– 1967	T	– 1980
H	– 1968	U	– 1981
I	– 1969	V	– 1982
J	– 1970	W	– 1983
K	– 1971	X	– 1984
L	– 1972	Y	– 1985
M	– 1973	Z	– 1986

Second letter (1961-86)
First letter (1987-96)

A	– January
B	– February
C	– March
D	– April
E	– May
F	– June
G	– July
H	– August
I/J	– September
J/K	– October
K/L	– November
L/M	– December

1987-1996
Prefix number = Year

0	– 1987
1	– 1988
2	– 1989
3	– 1990
4	– 1991
5	– 1992
6	– 1993
7	– 1994
8	– 1995
9	– 1996

For example: AA 47 – 1961 January
K6 5497 – November 1993

4003S/5 1986-current *Five strings.*
Similar to 4003S, except:
■ Five-string headstock, three-and-two
tuner arrangement.
■ Five-saddle bridge/tailpiece.
*Also 4003S/5/SPC BLACKSTAR with
black fingerboard and black-plated
hardware (1989).*

4003S/8 1986-current *Eight strings.*
Similar to 4003S, except:
■ Eight-string headstock, four-a-side
tuners.

4004C CHEYENNE 1993-current *Maple
through-neck, no pickguard, goldplated
hardware.*
■ All-maple through-neck; dot markers.
■ Unbound body; natural walnut wings.
■ Two controls (volume, tone) and three-
way selector, all mounted on body.
■ Gold-plated hardware.

4004L LAREDO 1994-current *Maple neck,
no pickguard, chrome-plated hardware.*
Similar to 4004C Cheyenne, except:
■ All-black body.
■ Chrome-plated hardware.

4008 1975-84 *Eight strings.*
Similar to 4001S (see earlier listing),
except:
■ Eight-string headstock, four-a-side
tuners.

Other basses produced by Rickenbacker include:

2020 Hamburg second version (1992-
current)
2030 Hamburg first version (1984-92)
2030GF Glenn Frey (1992-current)
2050 El Dorado first version (1984-92)
2060 El Dorado second version (1992-
current)
3000 (1975-84)
3001 (1975-84)
4005 (1965-84)
4005S (3261 in UK) (1965-69)
4005/6 six-string (1965-78)

ROLAND (Japan)

G-77 1985-86 *Spar connecting
headstock to angular offset body.*
■ Bolt-on neck with rosewood
fingerboard, dot markers; 34in scale,
21 frets; truss-rod adjuster at headstock
end; one string-guide; two-a-side tuners
with metal keys; four-screw neckplate.
■ Angular offset solid body,
headstock/body stabilizer spar; silver,
black or red.
■ Two pickups.
■ One large control (volume) six small
controls (pickup balance, tone, guitar/
synth balance, three for synth section)
and mini switch, all on body; side-
mounted jack and multi-pin synth
socket; active circuit.
■ Four-saddle bridge/tailpiece.
Also fretless version.

Other basses produced by Roland include:

G-33 (introduced 1980)
G-88 (introduced 1980)

SPECTOR

NS-2 1977-90 *Concave back/convex
front solid body, two pickups.*
■ Maple through-neck with rosewood
fingerboard, dot markers (later ornate);
34in scale; 24 frets; truss-rod adjuster
at headstock end; two-a-side tuners.
■ Carved double-cutaway solid body,
concave back/convex front; natural or
colors.
■ One split and one straight pickup.
■ Four controls (volume, two tone,
balance) and two mini switches, all
on body; side-mounted jack; active
circuit.
■ Four-saddle bridge/tailpiece.
*Also NS-1 with one pickup; three
controls (volume, two tone) and two
mini-switches (1977-82).*
*Also NS-1B and NS-2J bolt-on neck
versions (1982-85).*

Other basses produced by Spector include:

USA

SPECTOR SB-1 and SB-2 (1975-82)
SSD (Stuart Spector Design) NS-4 (1992-
current)
SSD (Stuart Spector Design) NS-5 (1993-
current)

CZECH REPUBLIC

**SSD (Stuart Spector Design) NS-4CR and
NS-5CR** (1995-current)

KOREA

NS series (1985-90)

STATUS (UK)

SERIES II 1985-95 *Headless graphite
neck, double cutaway body with long
hooked horns.*
■ Graphite through-neck with synthetic
fingerboard; 34in scale, 24 frets.
■ Contoured double-cutaway wood solid
body; natural.
■ Two pickups.
■ Four controls (volume, two tone,
balance) (later five controls – volume,
three tone, balance) mini switch and
jack, all on body; active circuit.
■ Four-saddle bridge and separate
tuner-tailpiece.
Also fretless, five-, and six-string versions.
Also STRATA brand versions (1982-84).

Other basses produced by Status include:

Eclipse series wood neck/body (introduced
1994)
Energy series wood neck/body (introduced
1991)
Series 2000 one-piece graphite
(introduced 1984)
Series 3000 graphite neck/wood body
(introduced 1987)
Series 4000 graphite neck/synthetic body
(introduced 1989)

STEINBERGER

Features common to all models, unless stated otherwise:
Headless synthetic neck.
Synthetic fingerboard.
Fretless fingerboard option.
Dot markers.
34in scale, 24 frets.
Solid body.
Plain-top pickups.
Controls all on body.
Side-mounted jack.
Four-saddle bridge/tuner-tailpiece.
Black-plated hardware.

USA

H-1 1980-82 *Body-top fixing bolts on front, one pickup.*
■ Synthetic one-piece neck/body (body with separate top); black.
■ One pickup.
■ Two controls (volume, tone).
■ Strap holder bracket on body back.
■ Hinged leg-rest on body side.

L-1 1980-84 *Body-top fixing bolts on front, one active pickup.*
Similar to H-1, except:
■ One active pickup.

H-2 1980-82 *Body-top fixing bolts on front, two pickups.*
■ Synthetic one-piece neck/body (body with separate top); black.
■ Two pickups.
■ Three controls (two volume, one tone).
■ Strap holder bracket on body back.
■ Hinged leg-rest on body side.

L-2 1980-84 *Body-top fixing bolts on front, two active pickups.*
Similar to H-2, except:
■ Two active pickups.
Replaced by XL-2 in 1984 (see later listing).
Also active tone circuit option (1982-84).

L-2/5 1982-84 *Body-top fixing bolts on front, five strings.*
Similar to L-2, except:
■ Five strings.
■ Five-saddle bridge/tuner-tailpiece.
Also active tone circuit option.

XL-2 1984-93 *Body-top fixing bolts on back, two active pickups.*
■ Synthetic one-piece neck/body (body with separate top); black or white.
■ Two active pickups.
■ Three controls (two volume, one tone).
■ Pivoting strap holder bracket on body back.
■ Hinged leg-rest on body side.
Replaced L-2 in 1984 and replaced by XL STANDARD in 1993 (see later listing).
Active tone circuit option; DB de-tuner bridge/tuner-tailpiece option (1990-93); TransTrem vibrato bridge/tuner-tailpiece option (1985-93).
Also XL-2DBA ELITE with active tone circuit, DB de-tuner bridge/tuner-tailpiece, gold Steinberger Elite logo (1992-93); replaced by XL ELITE in 1993 (see later listing).
Also XL-2GR with Roland GR synthesizer pickup, controls & circuit (1985-90).

XL-2/5 1984-93 *Body-top fixing bolts on back, five strings.*
Similar to XL-2, except:
■ Five strings.
■ Five-saddle bridge/tuner-tailpiece.
Replaced L-2/5 in 1984 and replaced by XL STANDARD 5 in 1993 (see later listing).
Also active tone circuit option.

XM-2 1986-93 *Bound double-cutaway wood body.*
■ Bolt-on synthetic neck; four-screw neckplate.
■ Bound double-cutaway wood body; black, white or red.
■ Two active pickups.
■ Three controls (two volume, one tone).

Also active tone circuit option; DB de-tuner bridge/tuner-tailpiece option (1990-93); TransTrem vibrato bridge/tuner-tailpiece option.

XQ-2 (also known as Q-4) 1990-93
Unbound contoured double-cutaway wood body.
■ Bolt-on synthetic neck; four-screw neckplate.
■ Unbound contoured double-cutaway wood body; black, white, red or blue.
■ Two active pickups.
■ Three controls (volume, tone, balance).
Also active tone circuit option; DB de-tuner bridge/tuner-tailpiece option; TransTrem vibrato bridge/tuner-tailpiece option.

XQ-2/5 (also known as Q-5) 1990-93
Unbound contoured double-cutaway wood body, five strings.
Similar to XQ-2 (Q-4), except:
■ Five strings.
■ Five-saddle bridge/tuner-tailpiece.
Also active tone circuit option.

XL STANDARD 1993-current *Two active pickups.*
■ Synthetic one-piece neck/body (body with separate top); black or white.
■ Two active pickups.
■ Three controls (volume, balance, treble/bass dual-concentric), active tone circuit.
■ Strap holder bracket on body back.
■ Hinged leg-rest on body side.
Replaced XL-2 in 1993 (see earlier listing).
Also XL ELITE with active tone circuit, DB de-tuner bridge/tuner- tailpiece, gold Steinberger Elite logo (1993-current); replaced XL-2DBA ELITE in 1993 (see earlier listing).
Also XL PRO with DB de-tuner bridge/tuner-tailpiece (1993-current).
Also TransTrem vibrato bridge/tuner-tailpiece option.

101

XL STANDARD 5 1993-current *Five strings.*
Similar to XL Standard, except:
■ Five strings.
■ Five-saddle bridge/tuner-tailpiece.
Replaced XL-2/5 in 1993 (see earlier listing).

XQ STANDARD 1993-current *Unbound double-cutaway wood body with slim left horn.*
■ Bolt-on synthetic neck; four-screw neckplate.
■ Unbound double-cutaway wood body; sunburst, natural or colors.
■ Two active pickups.
■ Three controls (volume, balance, treble/bass dual-concentric), active tone circuit.
Also XQ PRO with DB de-tuner bridge/tuner-tailpiece (1993-current).

XQ STANDARD 5 1993-current *Unbound double-cutaway wood body with slim left horn, five strings.*
Similar to XQ Standard, except:
■ Five strings.
■ Five-saddle bridge/tuner-tailpiece.

Other basses produced by Steinberger include:

JAPAN: STEINBERGER

XP-2 (1984-90)
XP-2/5 (1984-90)

KOREA: SPIRIT by STEINBERGER

XT-2 Spirit 4 (1993-current)
XT-2/5 Spirit 5 (1993-current)

TOBIAS (USA)

STANDARD V 1991-93. *Laminated through-neck, three controls.*
■ Laminated maple through-neck with rosewood fingerboard; 34in scale, 24 frets; truss-rod adjuster at body end; 'three-and-two' tuner arrangement.
■ Contoured double-cutaway solid body; natural or colors.

■ Two pickups.
■ Three controls (volume, balance, treble/ bass dual-concentric) all on body; side-mounted jack; active circuit.
■ Five-saddle bridge/tailpiece.
Also four-string and six-string versions.

Other basses produced by Tobias include:

Basic series (1984-current)
Classic series (1978-current)
Killer 'B' series (1991-current)
Signature series (1978-current)

TRAVIS BEAN (USA)

TB-2000 STANDARD 1976-79 *Aluminum neck with T-frame headstock.*
■ Bolt-on aluminum neck with rosewood fingerboard, dot markers; 34½in scale, 20 frets; T-frame headstock, two-a-side tuners.
■ Double-cutaway solid body; natural or colors.
■ Two metal-cover plain-top pickups.
■ Four controls (two volume, two tone) and three-way selector, all on body; side-mounted jack.
■ Four-saddle bridge with through-body stringing.

Other basses produced by Travis Bean include:

TB 4000 Wedge (1977-79)

TUNE (Japan)

BASS MANIAC 1983-current *25 frets.*
■ Bolt-on laminated maple neck with rosewood fingerboard, dot markers; 34in scale, 25 frets; truss-rod adjuster at headstock end; two-a-side tuners with metal keys.
■ Double-cutaway solid body; sunburst or colors.
■ One split pickup and one straight pickup.

■ Four controls (volume, two tone, balance) all on body; side-mounted jack; active circuit.
■ Four-saddle bridge/tailpiece.
Also five-string version.

Other basses produced by Tune include:

Bullseye series (1993-current)
GAP series (1989-92)
Somnus series (1987-94)
Syncron series (1988-92)
TWB series (1990-current)

VOX (Italy, UK)

STINGER IV 1968-70 *Teardrop-shape semi-solid.*
■ Bolt-on laminated maple neck with bound rosewood fingerboard, dot markers; 21 frets; truss-rod adjuster at body-end; two string-guides; four-in-line tuners with metal keys; four-screw neckplate.
■ Bound teardrop-shape semi-solid body, one f-hole; sunburst or red.
■ Two four-polepiece pickups.
■ Three controls (volume, two tone) and three-way selector, all on body; side-mounted jack.
■ Black laminated plastic pickguard.
■ Four-saddle bridge/tailpiece.

Other basses produced by Vox include:

Constellation IV active (introduced 1968)
Mark IV teardrop (introduced 1963)
Phantom IV (introduced 1962)

WAL (UK)

CUSTOM 1974-current *Double-cutaway contoured body; two pickups.*
■ Bolt-on laminated maple neck with rosewood fingerboard, dot markers; fretless ebony fingerboard option; 34in scale, 21 frets; truss-rod adjuster at body end; one or two string-guides;

two-a-side tuners with metal keys; four-screw neckplate.

▌ Contoured double-cutaway solid body; natural or colors.

▌ Two eight-polepiece pickups.

▌ Four controls (volume, two tone, balance) all on body; side-mounted jack and XLR socket; active circuit.

▌ Four-saddle bridge/tailpiece.

Earliest examples with five controls (three volume, two tone) and three-way selector, all on leather pickguard; non-active circuit.

Other basses produced by Wal include:

MIDI Bass (1987-current)
Pro I and Pro IE (1978-82)
Pro II and Pro IIE (1978-82)
Two-octave five-string (1986-current)
Two-octave four-string (1988-current)
Two-octave six-string (1994-current)

WARWICK (Germany)

THUMB 1985-current *Laminated through-neck, 26 frets, two pickups.*

▌ Laminated through-neck with wenge fingerboard (ebony option), dot markers; fretless ebony fingerboard option; 34in scale, 26 frets; truss-rod adjuster at headstock end; two-a-side tuners with metal keys.

▌ Carved double-cutaway solid body, concave back/convex front; natural.

▌ Two pickups.

▌ Three controls (volume, balance, treble/bass dual-concentric) later volume, balance/middle dual-concentric) all on body; side-mounted jack; active circuit.

▌ Four-saddle bridge/tailpiece (later four-saddle bridge and separate tailpiece).

Also five-string and six-string versions.
Also bolt-on neck versions.

Other basses produced by Warwick include:

Buzzard (1986-current)
Corvette Pro Line series (1992-current)
Dolphin Pro I series (1989-current)
Fortress series (1993-current)
Nobby Meidel (1982-90)
Streamer series (1984-current)

YAMAHA (Japan/Taiwan)

BB-5000 1984-88 *Five-string, through-neck with oval markers, one split and one straight pickup in metal surrounds.*

▌ Laminated maple through-neck with ebony fingerboard, oval markers; 33⅞in scale, 24 frets; truss-rod adjuster at body end; one string-guide; 'four-and-one' tuner arrangement.

▌ Contoured double-cutaway solid body; colors.

▌ One split pickup and one straight pickup.

▌ Two controls (volume, tone) and three-way selector, all on body; side-mounted jack.

▌ Five-saddle bridge/tailpiece.

▌ Gold-plated hardware.

Replaced by BB-5000A with four controls (volume, two tone, balance); active circuit (1988-92). Also BB-5000AF with fretless ebony fingerboard (1989-92).

Other basses produced by Yamaha include:

Attitude series (introduced 1990)
BB series (introduced 1978)
MB series (introduced 1986)
RBX series (introduced 1986)
TRB series (introduced 1989)

Yamaha Serial Numbers

We can't help you date Japanese output, but Taiwan-made basses since 1984 usually have a two-letter/five-figure serial where the first letter reveals the instrument's age:

K	– 1984	Q	– 1990
L	– 1985	R	– 1991
M	– 1986	S	– 1992
N	– 1987	T	– 1993
O	– 1988	U	– 1994
P	– 1989	V	– 1995

For example: PZ3472 – 1989

ZEMAITIS (UK)

Most Zemaitis instruments were, and still are, custom-built to order, and these include a small selection of basses.

ZON (USA)

MICHAEL MANRING HYPERBASS VERSION II
1990-current *Extended fretless neck, body with extra-deep cutaway.*

▌ Glued-in graphite extended (three octave) neck with synthetic fretless fingerboard; 34in scale; two-a-side tuners with metal keys and tuning extenders.

▌ Double-cutaway solid body; natural or colors.

▌ One pickup.

▌ Three controls (volume, tone, balance) all on body; side-mounted jack; active circuit.

▌ Four-saddle bridge/re-tuner tailpiece.

▌ Black-plated hardware.

Also Version I without re-tuning facility.
Also Version III with re-tuning facility; piezo pickups in body and neck with associated controls.

Other basses produced by Zon include:

Legacy series (1981-current)
Scepter (1984-93)
Sonus (1991-current)

103

107

OWNERS' CREDITS

Guitars photographed came from the following individuals' collections, and we are most grateful for their help.

The owners are listed here in the alphabetical order of the code used to identify their guitars in the Key To Guitar Photographs below.
AJ Anthony Jackson; **AM** Albert Molinaro; **ARO** Alan Rogan; **ARU** Allan Russell; **BC** Bass Centre London; **BD** Bob Daisley; **CC** The Chinery Collection; **CH** Colin Hodgkinson; **CN** Carl Nielsen; **CS** Chris Squire; **DBE** Dave Brewis; **DBO** Dave Bronze; **DQ** Danny Quatrochi; **FF** Fausto Fabi; **GE** Giddy-Up-Einstein; **GF** Guitar Factory; **GG** Geoff Gould; **GL** G&L; **GP** Guy Pratt; **GU** Guitars R Us; **HK** Hap Kuffner; **HR** Hard Rock Cafe London; **JA** Jeff Allen; **JB** Jack Bruce; **JE** John Entwistle; **JG** John Gustafson; **JR** Jim Roberts; **JS** John Slog; **JZ** Joe Zon; **KR** Keith Robertson; **MA** Michael Anthony; **MF** Mo Foster; **MG** Merv Goldsworthy; **MK** Mark King; **MM** Marcus Miller; **MP** Maurice Preece; **OM** Omec; **PD** Paul Day; **PM** Paul McCartney; **PPA** Pino Palladino; **PPE** Philip Pell; **PW** Paul Westwood; **RF** Rock Factory; **SC** Stanley Clarke; **SP** Steve Partlett; **SS** Steve Soest.

KEY TO BASS GUITAR PHOTOGRAPHS

The following key is designed to identify who owned which basses when they were photographed for this book. After the relevant page number (*in italic type*) we list: the brand, model or other identifier, followed by the owner's initials in **bold type** (see Owners' Credits above). For example, '*10*: Precision 1951 **JE**' means that the 1951 Precision shown on page 10 was owned by John Entwistle.

Jacket front: Alembic Mark King 1994 **BC**; Jazz Bass 1963 **JA**. *Inside front jacket flap:* Ampeg ASB-1 c1967 **JE**. *2/3:* Music Man StingRay Bass 1976 **SP**; Rickenbacker 4001S 1964 **PD**. *6/7:* Jazz Bass 1974 **JE**. *11:* both **BD**. *14/15:* Left-hand Höfner **PM**; right-hand Höfner **BC**; Danelectro six-string **PPE**. *14:* Gibson with spike **JS**, without **JE**. *15:* Rickenbacker 4000 **MA**. *18/19:* EB-2 **BD**. *19:* Framus **BD**. *19:* Harmony **MP**; Epiphone **BD**. *22/23:* Rickenbacker 4001 **JS**; EB-3 **DBE**. *23:* Fender VI **JE**; Gretsch **BC**. *25/26:* Burns **KR**; Danelectro Long Horn **SS**. *26:* Thunderbird IV **JE**; Thunderbird II **AM**; Vox **CN**. *27/28/29:* Jazz white **ARU**. *28/29:* Jazz burgundy **GP**. *29:* Jazz natural **MM**. *32:* Bass V **BC**; Ampeg AEB-1 **FF**. *33:* Guild Starfire **JR**; Rickenbacker 4001S **PM**. *36:* Les Paul Bass **RF**; Hagstrom **BC**; Precision Fretless **BC**. *37:* Ampeg Dan Armstrong **CC**; Mustang **BC**. *40/41:* Alembic #001 **GE**; Alembic tenor **SC**; Alembic eight **HR**. *41:* Alembic Spider **JE**. *44/45:* Spector **AM**; Kramer **MF**. *45:* BC Rich **MA**; Earthwood **JE**; Travis Bean **GU**. *47/48:* Aria **BC**; Ibanez **DQ**. *48:* Wal triple-neck **CH**; StingRay fretless **PPA**. *49/50/51:* G&L L2000 **GF**; Leo's test bass **GL**; Sabre **BC**. *54/55:* Carl Thompson **CH**; Steinberger prototype model **HK**; Jaydee **MK**. *55:* Steinberger production model **BC**; Status **BC**. *58/59:* Fodera **AJ**; Modulus **GG**. *59:* Ken Smith **BC**; Tobias **BC**; Yamaha **MG**. *62/63:* Warwick **JB**; Hamer **KR**; Kubicki **JZ**. *63:* Roland **MA**. *66:* Overwater **JE**; Tune **BC**; Ashbory **PW**. *67:* Pedulla **BC**; Zemaitis **JA**. *70/71:* Steinberger Q4 **OM**; Steinberger XM2 **BC**; Ovation **DBO**. *71:* Kramer Ferrington **BC**; Martin **JR**. *74/75:* G&L prototype **GL**; Peavey **BC**. *75:* Zon **JZ**. *Jacket back:* Steinberger **BC**.

Bass guitar photography was by Garth Blore, Nigel Bradley and Miki Slingsby.

MEMORABILIA illustrated in this book, including catalogs, brochures, magazines, record sleeves and photographs (in fact anything that isn't a bass) came from the collections of Alembic, Tony Bacon, *Bass Player*, Paul Day, *Guitar Player*, Barry Moorhouse, Philip Pell, Rickenbacker, St Louis Music and Steve Soest. These finely textured items were transformed for your enjoyment by Miki Slingsby. The photo of Chris Squire on p33 is reproduced by kind permission of the photographer, Miki Slingsby. The photo of Jimmy Johnson on p58 is reproduced by kind permission of the photographer, Margot Reyes.

INTERVIEWS

We are very grateful to the many individuals who consented to be interviewed for this book. Unsourced quotations in the text are from original interviews conducted (unless stated) between November 1994 and January 1995 especially for *The Bass Book*. Interviews with the following were conducted by Tony Bacon: Dave Bronze (April 1994); Rick Danko; Nathan East (January 1992); Danny Ferrington; George Fullerton (February 1992); John Hall; Dale Hyatt; Ted McCarty (October 1992); Jaco Pastorius (July 1976); Don Randall; Forrest White (February 1992). Interviews with the following were conducted by Tony Bacon & Barry Moorhouse: Steve Chick; Nathan Daniel; Vinnie Fodera; Geoff Gould; Anthony Jackson; Jimmy Johnson; Dennis Kager; Paul McCartney; Jess Oliver; Ken Smith; Stuart Spector; Ned Steinberger; Carl Thompson; Rick Turner; Ron Wickersham. The quotations on page 17 by Monk Montgomery from the 1980 interview conducted by Maggie Hawthorn are from the Institute Of Jazz Studies archive at Rutgers, the State University of New Jersey. The sources of other previously published quotations are given where they occur in the text.

IN ADDITION to those named above in OWNERS' CREDITS and in INTERVIEWS we would like to thank: American Federation of Musicians (Los Angeles, Nashville, New York); Dennis Anthony; Bob Archigian (LaBella); Jez Ayscough (House Music); Paul Bechtoldt; Bob Bernstein (Hard Rock); Andrew Bodnar; Bruce Bolen; Julie Bowie; Russell Bowner (Hard Rock London); Craig Brody; Boz Burrell; Dave Burrluck (*Guitar Magazine*); Calloway Editions; Mike Carey; Walter Carter (Gibson); Trevor Cash; Scott Chinery; Craig DeFalco; André Duchossoir; Howard Fields; Vinnie Fodera; Roger Forrester; Bert Gerecht; Dave Good (House Music); Martin Gravestock (Bass Centre London); Alan Greenwood; John Hammel; Rick Harrison (Music Ground); Steve Hodgkinson; Stan Jay (Mandolin Bros); Scott Jennings (Route 66 Guitars); Chris Jisi; Bill Kaman; Dixie Kidd; Lagavulin; Dan Lakin; Scott Malandrone; John McLaren Jnr (G&L); Tony Moscal (St Louis Music); Gill Moorhouse; Hans Moust; National Association of Music Merchants; New York Public Library for the Performing Arts; Jim Otell; Nick Owen (Bass Centre London); Vincent Pelote (Institute of Jazz Studies, Rutgers); Bob Pridden; Russell Prince (House Music); Ian Purser; Heinz Rebellius: Rob Rizzuto (G&L); Howard Satterley; Martin Scott (MPL); Maggie Simpson (*Melody Maker*); Keith Smith; Pete 'The Fish' Stevens (Wal); Ray Todd (Strings & Things); Rob Turner (EMG); Bud Tutmarc; Ariana Urbont (MTV); Chris Ward (Bass Centre London); Mica Wickersham (Alembic).

SPECIAL THANKS to: Paul Day for admirably filling the rear of this pantomime horse (aka Reference Section); Jim Roberts for consistent support and help above and beyond the international dateline; Steve Soest for checking here, there and everywhere each Tuesday (hi Amy!); and Sally Stockwell for making all those funny shapes look as if they were made for one another.

BIBLIOGRAPHY

Ken Achard *The Fender Guitar* (Musical New Servides 1977); Tony Bacon & Lawrence Canty *What Bass* (Track Record 1992); Tony Bacon & Paul Day *The Fender Book* (IMP/Miller Freeman 1992), *The Gibson Les Paul Book* (IMP/Miller Freeman 1993), *The Rickenbacker Book* (IMP/Miller Freeman 1994), *The Ultimate Guitar Book* (DK/Knopf 1991); Paul Bechtholdt *G&L: Leo's Legacy* (Woof 1994); *Bizarre Guitars* (Rittor 1993); Klaus Blasquiz *The Fender Bass* (Hal Leonard undated); André Duchossoir *Gibson Electrics – The Classic Years* (Hal Leonard 1994); George Fullerton *Guitar Legends* (Centerstream 1993); Bert Gerecht *Bass Talk!* (Bund 1991); Ira Gershwin *Lyrics* (Elm Tree 1977); George Gruhn & Walter Carter *Gruhn's Guide To Vintage Guitars* (GPI 1991); Terry Hounsome *Rock Record 4* (RRP 1991); Ernst Jorgensen et al *Elvis Recording Sessions* (Jee 1984); Colin Larkin (editor) *The Guinness Encyclopedia Of Popular Music* (Guinness 1992); Mark Lewisohn *The Complete Beatles Recording Sessions* (Hamlyn 1988), *The Complete Beatles Chronicle* (Pyramid 1992); Dr Licks *Standing In The Shadows Of Motown* (Dr Licks 1989); Dave Marsh *Before I Get Old* (Plexus 1983); Willie G Moseley *Stellas & Stratocasters* (Vintage Guitar Books 1994); Tom Mulhern (editor) *Bass Heroes* (GPI 1993); Norm N Nite *Rock On Almanac* (HarperPerennial 1992); Michael Ochs *Rock Archives* (Blandford 1985); Norbert Schnepel & Helmut Lemme *Elektro-Gitarren Made In Germany* English translation J P Klink (Musik-Verlag Schnepel-Lemme 1988); Tom Wheeler *American Guitars* (HarperPerennial 1990); Forest White *Fender The Inside Story* (GPI 1994).

We also consulted back issues of the following magazines: *Bass* (Japan); *Bass Player* (US); *Beat Instrumental* (UK); *Beat Monthly* (UK); *Down Beat* (US); *GQ* (US); *Guitar Magazine* (UK); *Guitar Player* (US); *Guitarist* (UK); *Innovation, The Journal of the Industrial Designers Society of America*; *Making Music* (UK); *Melody Maker* (UK); *Mojo* (UK); *Record Collector* (US); *The Music Trades* (US); *Rolling Stone* (US); *Vintage Gallery* (US); *Vintage Guitar Magazine* (US); *20th Century Guitar* (US).

"Everything that can be invented has been invented." Charles H Duell, Commissioner of US Patent Office, 1899.

108